2.25

Polymer Painting

and related techniques

WAYNESBORO, PA. by Paul Sarkisian. Medium: Acrylic on canvas (various brands). (Courtesy: the artist. Photograph by Frank J. Thomas, Los Angeles, Calif.) The air brush has been used by several artists in recent years to achieve the Super-real image. West Coast artist Paul Sarkisian produces huge paintings of almost *beyond-photo-realism* in *beyond-the-real colors.* Multiple coats of very thin polymer are sprayed onto a carefully gessoed canvas, sometimes using yellow under red or red under blue to achieve unusual, vibrant color. In this way a luminosity and intensity is produced that is hard to duplicate with brushed color. The hard edges and outlines are masked out with tape during the spraying process. For other spray techniques see pages 21, 51, 60-62.

Polymer Painting

and related techniques

Russell O. Woody, Jr.

with course outline and works of prominent artists

VNR VAN NOSTRAND REINHOLD COMPANY

NEW YORK CINCINNATI TORONTO LONDON MELBOURNE

This book is dedicated to Penelope, Luranah, Leona

ACKNOWLEDGMENTS

The author is greatly indebted to the artists whose
work appears in this book. They have spent time and
energy and given advice and friendship without
which this book would not have been possible.

Also I will always be indebted to Henry W.
Levison, chemist and president of Permanent
Pigments, Inc., who has offered his advice and
encouragement over the years and who has been a
long suffering teacher, mentor, and friend. Without
his contributions to the fields of artist's polymers and
color chemistry and without his freely given
knowledge and advice to artists I doubt if the polymer
emulsion paints would be as advanced as they are at
this point in history.

Special credit should also be given to artist and
teacher, George Chavatel for his advice on teaching
outlines; to artist and teacher Toby Joysmith and the
late José Gutiérrez who encouraged my first forays
into polymer painting; and to Mrs. Sue Salmon for
her help in physically putting this book together at
times when it seemed impossible.

Also by Russell O. Woody, Jr.
PAINTING WITH SYNTHETIC MEDIA
Technical appendix by Henry W. Levison

CONTENTS

(Continued overleaf)

COLOR ILLUSTRATIONS

This is a book devoted to the explanation of polymer emulsion techniques and materials. It is not a primer on composition, perspective, and pretty palette arrangements, or esthetics. There are innumerable books covering these subjects; the reader should refer to them if he wants an ABZ, step-by-step approach on "how to paint a picture." It is not the purpose of this book to show anyone how to approach a painting from a specific point of view, but it will describe how your own approach can be accomplished with a new standard in artists' materials: polymer emulsions.

To understand what polymers are and what their far-reaching possibilities may be, it is necessary to have a cursory understanding of what is happening now, and what might happen in the future to painting media.

Our world today is a world of change and speed; of almost daily shifts in social, economic, religious, and political structures. The mass, the group, has many times replaced the individual. In this milieu, mass media has evolved and media has become the message, or the massage. Spanning the many dichotomies of modern life is the steady, forceful, almost relentless, march of an expanding technology.

A decade ago the artist was aware of, and more or less influenced by, the changes going on but was not aware of the technology—if he bothered to look to the areas of chemistry, physics, or the industrial sciences at all. This is no longer the case. The artist has linked the rush of world change with that of technology, and the pace of art—as well as that of life—has increased. The number of artists that have so suddenly embraced technological developments increases; and with their explorations the shape, feel, and look of art alters from day to day. Traditional media as we have known them will be replaced. Oil painting, which has dominated the art scene for the past 400 years, will soon be of secondary importance, possibly within fifteen years, I believe, and eventually may be relegated to a position somewhat like that of true fresco today; it may be used for specific purposes but not generally.

Out of the development and search for better and more empathetic media one constant has emerged: polymers in general, and polymer emulsions in particular. I think that polymer emulsions herald the new art media of the future, are a bridge between the traditional and the new media approach, and will remain a dominant media for many years to come.

There are many reasons for my belief. First, and most practical, is the fact that polymer emulsions are now easy to obtain; every artists' materials manufacturer offers a polymer emulsion brand and many new companies are entering the field, in some cases producing only polymer emulsions. The path of least resistance is followed by most manufacturers. This is in contrast to the constant search, research, and experimentation with which the earlier devotees of synthetic media had to contend, and which, as often as not, proved to be blind and disastrous groping.

Another practical consideration is demand. Although some of the statements I made only four years ago regarding the displacement of traditional paints by synthetic media were considered by many to be gross exaggerations, today at least half the young artists now use polymers in every phase of artistic creation, from traditional and modern painting through constructions and graphics (collagraphs) to sculpture. Many colleges and universities as well as public school systems now *require* polymers to be used by the student. Approximately a third of the college art departments now introduce the student to polymer collagraphs. The word "polymer" is commonly seen attached to paintings, reproductions, and whole shows. Demand did not come first in the development of polymer emulsions. When they became commercially available, over twelve years ago, as a complete range of painting media, technically aware artists adopted polymer emulsions and their use grew steadily and rapidly.

Second, polymer emulsions offer almost unlimited versatility, and for this reason most artists and schools have adopted the medium. Almost any technique accomplished with traditional media can be visually duplicated with polymer emulsions. They can be used as a *better* oil medium. That is, they can duplicate all the vaunted visual effects of oils—the rich hues, the vast range of textures, impastos, and glazes, the air of "presence" and "importance"—but in a much freer and more comfortable handling technique and with the promise of far greater durability. New developments have produced a new polymer emulsion with even the "feel," the "push and pull," and a similar viscosity to that of oil paint.

Polymer emulsion paints can also be used to emulate the effects of watercolor, casein, tempera, egg tempera, or gouache. They are well-suited for true fresco techniques, painting directly into wet plaster, or for *fresco secco*. The paints plus polymer mediums make a direct, brush-applied silk-screen blockout, and they can be used as the silk-screen ink and as a limited ink for wood-block prints. Printed or applied directly to cloth they are a durable textile paint. The polymer medium is a good fixative for charcoal, chalk, and pastel and is an excellent glue, comprising the first sensible material for making collages that will not collapse or disintegrate within a few years.

As a plate-building material, the various polymer products have given a new direction to the area of prints. Polymer emulsion pastes and cements can be built into large sculptural mass, used for jewelry and innumerable craft projects to simulate the surface quality of stone, wood, or almost anything desired. And more. The major portion of this book is devoted to how these techniques are accomplished.

Third, and perhaps the most important, the polymer emulsions open a whole new world of esthetic expression. They have characteristics of their own that artists still have only begun to exploit. The polymer emulsions particularly exhibit a brilliance, a luminosity, and a transparency of color previously unknown in any artists' medium. Their adaptability to new forms is inherent, and the material in itself many times initiates exploration and excitement.

Fourth, polymer emulsions are a fast-working, fast-drying material. This fact has been quoted as a disadvantage as often as it has been quoted as an advantage. To me and to most of those using polymer emulsions, it is the material's best quality. Because it does require quick reaction on the part of the artist, it is especially geared to the pace of today's high-speed, complex society and has a direct effect in recreating this quality in the esthetic approach. It also requires skill on the part of the artist and forces the student to master good technique immediately. One has to be good, or else one is very quickly and very permanently wrong. For the same reason polymer emulsions are good teaching materials: what oil technique requires to be done in three months can be accomplished in three days with polymer emulsions.

This also means a greater output for the fine artist and is especially advantageous for the commercial artist—very simply, he is more creative or makes more money. The material also makes one think; you have to know what you are about before slapping on the paint. This isn't such a bad approach, once one becomes accustomed to the thought process.

Fifth, polymer emulsions are relatively inexpensive. When all things are considered—basic cost of paints, supports, versatility, handling, etc. —the overall cost of using polymer emulsion colors is less than half the cost of using oil paints. Of course, if they are compared to a school-grade tempera and if they are used to replace only one material, such as tempera, polymers will be more expensive. However, with this minor exception, the one factor of low cost makes them highly desirable to schools, especially to the art students.

Sixth, all tests indicate that polymers, when properly handled and of high quality materials, offer greater durability than any other medium in the history of art, including oils. The colors, suspended as they are in a medium of utter transparency, will not discolor or yellow with age if the paint is correctly formulated. The film that forms over the painting is an almost indestructable surface that will not crack, or flake, or show signs of aging.

Finally, there is a historic continuity, which polymer emulsions afford. This is the reason I have said that this media will remain a dominant one for years to come. Although the phrase "historic continuity" may seem heretical to some artists working in the further out modern approaches, and may also appear to be antithetical to some of my own statements, it may be balm to others. The assertion has a deep basis in the fact that artists, until very recently, have been among the most conservative of people where the mechanics of their craft are concerned.

These artists, these "antennae of the future," these "freely inventive and courageous iconclasts" took almost two hundred years to completely accept oil paint as a "universal" medium, and have now just begun to exploit certain types of polymers developed in the late 1930's, as well as the vinyl and acrylic emulsions developed in the 40's and 50's! Of course I agree that the exploration of craft, as well as art itself, needs to encompass the past, but it should not be confined by it. Polymer emulsions offer this possibility. They can be used to duplicate the processes of Rembrandt, or to forge boldly into the Color Field, the Op and Primary structures of now. The artist or student is free to develop as closely to the historical stream as he wishes, or as far from it as his tributary flows.

Many outstanding artists have turned to polymers, and their influence is great. They included Magic Realists, Abstract Expressionists, Op and Pop artists, Hard Edge painters, the New Realists, Psychedelics, and commercial artists. Among them are Boris Artzybasheff, Arnold Belkin, Thomas Hart Benton, James Brooks, Gene Davis, Ron Davis, Allan D'Arcangelo, Elaine deKooning, Helen Frankenthaler, Robert Goodnough, Adolph Gottlieb, Al Held, Charles Hinman, Raymond Jonson, Toby Joysmith, Yeves Klein, Nicholas Krushenick, Alfred Leslie, Morris Lewis, Leo Manso, Marisol, Barnett Newman, Kenneth Noland, Gabor Peterdi, Larry Poons, Fairfield Porter, Milton Resnick, Richard Smith, Syd Soloman, Ernest Trova, and Karl Zerbe.

It can safely be said that all the boundaries of art have finally been demolished—if not for the public, at least for the artist. Works of art not only include paint and canvas, stone and wood, but moving parts, light, sound, and found materials of innumerable kinds. The performing arts have joined the plastic arts and these areas have council with technical engineers. Size is large to minimal. Space is defined by size and shape, or there is transparently defined space—glass or clear polymers. Polymer emulsions, it can be seen, are not the only answer when the door to speculation about the future is opened.

In 1966, at the Graham Gallery in New York, there was a show of "abstract inflationism" with many works done with stuffed or inflated plastics and canvas, covered with polymer emulsions. Some of these pieces were six feet high to four feet wide, yet could be deflated to approximately two-by-four-by-four inches. In the small size they are easily transportable and then can be blown up (abstract *inflationism*) to produce a sculptural mass.

This may solve one of today's problems of shifting population—one out of every four families moves every year in the United States. Now you can "take it with you" with minimal shipping problems; just carry a houseful of sculpture in a handbag or your pockets.

Another development could bring the whole of art work into your home. The development of the laser beam is in its infancy, but one of its uses has far-reaching possibilities for the artist: the hologram. When a laser beam is projected through a photograph taken on a hologram film, a three-dimensional image of an object in actual space can be projected. The individual can see the object in three-dimensions and view it from all sides and angles as though the object were in reality there. The hologram is not perfected for home use as yet, but it will be.

Another aspect of this direction is the holograph, whereby an artist could scratch or paint directly onto special film and have his work projected in three dimensions. He could literally paint or draw in space. The laser projection could lead to transforming the boob tube into a new mass media art form. TV projection could encompass the room, enabling the viewer to become part of, or stand in, or move around in the three-dimensional projection: a happening in which the viewer is involved. Possibilities along this line of speculation are limitless. It could also eliminate art as we know it (art as an object). Today, multiple and interrelated light, sound, film, and slide projections already forecast this direction of total involvement.

The computer can also serve the will of the artist. Artists are working with expandable foaming synthetics such as polyurethane. Of course some of today's artists do only the rough sketch or diagram of their work and send this out to industrial craftsmen to construct.

The artist and teacher of the future may be nothing like we envision. He may need to be a chemist as well as a computer programmer, or he may just mix pills as he now mixes paint. Pills do almost everything today and we may move into a new phase of *Brave New World* by popping in a pill to experience whatever we want to experience: from preventing conception to creating concepts. Art would then be total involvement of the individual, internally producing not only color and shape but controlling moods and states of mind: LSD-related halucigenics under control.

A discussion of this sort could go on forever.

Whether these directions are good or bad is to be determined by the artists following them. Polymer emulsions may seem very tame in comparison, more traditional than new. But polymer emulsions are the forerunner of all that is to come. They are the perfected medium of the future, now.

To a certain extent, the behavior of polymer emulsion paints requires new methods of working. In general, these new techniques are easier than those required by traditional media, and they minimize the artist's concern about technical or mechanical matters. But this does not mean there are no rules for painting with polymer emulsions. There are, and the artist must know them well if he wants his tools to work for him and not against him. New materials and new directions demand new technical approaches.

The more esoteric synthetics, such as lacquers, polyesters, ethyl silicates, etc., have been omitted from this book because of the now limited interest in them. Owing to their uncertain durability and their technical limitations, they have been replaced by polymer emulsions or newer synthetics. If the reader is interested in other synthetics for painting, he is referred to *Painting With Synthetic Media* (Van Nostrand Reinhold) by the author; or if he is interested in synthetics for sculptural purposes, he should consult *Plastics as an Art Form* by Thelma Newman or *Sculpture in Plastic* by Nicholas Roukes.

The purpose of this book is to explain the nature and the behavior of polymer emulsions, to survey the varieties available to the artist, to discuss how these paints may be used in actual operation, and to illustrate their diverse manipulations by the nature of my own work and that of other artists. The techniques described need not be the only ones the artist may employ. The potentials are endless, and I would encourage the reader—once he has a basic understanding of the composition, behavior, and physical characteristics of the materials—to explore and experiment for himself. Here is a medium for your message—or anti-message.

1

Basic Terms, Structure, and Character

Polymer emulsions are no longer new; they have been produced now for over fourteen years as a commercial paint and medium for the fine artist, and artists have used them an even longer period of time, formulating their own paints. The use of synthetics as art media started with the Mexican Muralists as early as 1930 and has continued until today. In the late 1930's acrylic resins were produced commercially and this polymer type has become dominant in the past ten years, as an emulsion of the acrylic in water. We now have extensive information available and a relatively long period of use and experimentation directly applicable to the fine arts and we can, therefore, make some fairly safe rules and statements about polymers as an art medium.

However, to understand what these materials are, what their advantages may be, and how they are used, it is necessary to review some basic terms in relation to how these terms relate to polymers in general and polymer emulsions in particular.

The Structure of Paint. All paints, from tempera to oil to watercolor to synthetics, are composed of two essential ingredients: *pigment,* which is a dry, powdery substance that provides the color in a paint; and *medium,* which is a liquid vehicle in which the pigment is suspended and by which the pigment is applied and adhered to a surface.

(Other materials are often added to paints for a variety of reasons, to give body and fluidity, to achieve matte or gloss effects, etc., but pigments and media are the essentials.)

Traditional paints, such as oils and watercolors, use natural resins for media. Linseed oil, the basis for oil media, is an oil pressed from the seeds of the flax plant and purified for use. The synthetic paints, however, use artificially created chemical products for media called *synthetic resins* and in the fine arts field are referred to generally as *polymers.*

Definition of Polymer Emulsion Media. An *emulsion* is the suspension of a finely divided material in a liquid. A "polymer emulsion"—also called "polymer tempera" some years ago—is a synthetic emulsion created by suspending minute particles of polymer resin in water. This suspension is achieved by *polymerizing* the resin while it is suspended in water, not by just mixing a polymer resin in water. When *monomers* (which are basic chemical units—rather small molecules) are chemically joined the result is an extremely long chain consisting of thousands of these basic units. At this point we have a large or "giant" molecular structure called a *polymer.* The term polymerization refers to the process of forming large molecules from smaller molecules.

Monomer means "one part" (taken from the Greek word *monos*), and polymer means "many parts." Considering it this way may simplify the terms for the reader.

When monomers (usually liquids) are suspended and polymerized in water we have a *polymer emulsion:* solid, minute particles of polymer resin suspended in water. This is a more complicated chemical process than the simple physical one of pressing oil out of flax seed but it yields a medium that is substantially more appropriate for making a better paint. It also allows for a wide variety of media for specific purposes by varying the monomeric components. It is also highly confusing to the layman. So let us be very simple and say a polymer emulsion is the suspension of a plastic (polymer resin) in water.

Manufacturing a Polymer Emulsion Paint. If color pigments are suspended along with the resin in an emulsion, a paint is formed. The water provides fluidity for the medium and when the water evaporates the resin particles flow together to form a strong, coherent film of plastic, which binds the pigment particles together. The paint film is water insoluble—it cannot be redissolved in water—but it is not water impervious, because there are microscopic holes between the plastic particles, which, in thin films, allow the film to breathe.

The grinding of pigments into a polymer emulsion is not a simple matter of pouring in a bit of color and stirring. As with oil paints, each pigment requires a different amount of medium to produce a good paste with correct brushing qualities. For most colors the same pigments are used in polymer emulsions as in oil paints. Some traditional pigments, however, such as Viridian and Alizarin Crimson, cannot be used correctly in certain types of polymer emulsions because the emulsion may be alkaline in its liquid form (such as acrylics) and will react with the pigment. Therefore, new synthetic pigments are used and you may have to learn some new color names such as Linear Quinacridone Violet, Naphthol ITR Crimson, or Dioxazine Purple. Until your tongue becomes accustomed to these new sounds, there are color charts and you can point.

Other chemicals, such as wetting agents, dispersing agents, preservatives, and thickeners, are added to polymer emulsions to stabilize the resin particles and pigments (that is, keep them in suspension) and to produce proper handling qualities, etc.

Types of Polymer Emulsion. There are hundreds of polymer types available today. The broad generic term that should be used for all types that are water soluble in their liquid state is *polymer emulsion.* They should not be lumped together under the heading of *acrylics.* This is a misnomer that has developed because most companies produce acrylic polymer paints for the artist. It is important for the artist to know which type of polymer emulsion he is using, because each type has its own characteristics. Here are a few rules that should be observed in relation to the type used.

Three general types of polymer emulsion paints are produced for the artist today, and in the future there may be more. Those most widely used have an *acrylic* resin base. Those with a *polyvinyl acetate* base were used in the early stages of emulsion development. They are also generally known as "vinyls" or PVA. PVA paints have largely been superseded by what are known in the paint trade as *copolymers.* In the paint trade, when similar monomers or monomers of the same family (i.e. different acrylic monomers) are polymerized together, they form a polymer. When two monomers of **DIFFERENT** chemical families are polymerized together, the result is a copolymer (a *copolymerization* process). The most common combination of different chemical families is that of acrylic and vinyl to form a *vinyl-acrylic copolymer emulsion.*

Comparison of Polymer Emulsion Types. Most acrylic resins are inherently highly flexible. Over a prolonged period of time most polyvinyl acetate resins will become slightly brittle, and the additives used with PVA resins to increase their adhesiveness will often turn yellow. It is easy to see

12

that from the artist's standpoint PVA should be avoided. Since all the white, water-soluble glues I have seen on the market today are PVA emulsions, it follows that these glue emulsions should be shunned by the artist who wants durability for more than a few years. They are good glues but not fine arts materials. To make a polyvinyl acetate flexible enough for durability, various proportions of acrylic chemicals or other chemicals are incorporated in the formulation of the resin polymer to form a copolymer.

Acrylic emulsions are alkaline, chemically, while PVA emulsions and copolymer emulsions are usually acidic. Therefore, most of the different emulsion types and paints will chemically react with one another and should not be mixed together in their liquid state. Sometimes these reactions are violent and cause glutinous masses, "jelly" or just plain stringy gunk that the artist cannot use. When the polymer emulsions dry, they are chemically inert and therefore can be painted one over the other with comparative safety. However, it is best to paint with one type of polymer emulsion or, better yet, to paint only with one specific brand of polymer emulsion paint. If this is done, and the paint brand is a correctly formulated one, the artist is on a much sounder basis than chancing even marginal reactions or poor adhesion between competing brands, which is sometimes hard for the artist to detect. (See also **Testing**, page 30.)

Advantages as a Paint Medium. Pigment may be considered the substance or the objective of a painting, and medium, as its name implies is a means to an end. All media should meet a certain basic list of requirements in order to serve the pigment well and to perform satisfactorily. There are many clear cut advantages of polymer emulsions over traditional painting media. Among them are the following, which are especially applicable to the acrylics:

1. High elasticity, thus permitting maximum flexibility, expansion, and contraction in paint films (unless the film is manipulated while frozen).

2. Colorless transparency. They do not impose a color of their own nor yellow with age.

3. Fast drying with no prolonged chemical drying action. Almost immediate overpainting and varnishing is possible.

4. Great adhesiveness to most painting supports.

5. Higher degree of light reflection and refraction than oils, thus giving more brilliance of color.

6. High resistance to ultra violet light (which causes pigments to fade) imparts a longer life to the pigment.

7. They form a permanent protective film for the pigment, thus preserving the life of a painting.

8. They give excellent dispersion of pigment.

9. They are nontoxic.

10. They allow a greater versatility of technique than any other medium.

11. Water soluble when wet. While wet, they can be easily cleaned from brushes with only soap and water.

12. There are no objectional odors, fumes, or vapors to permeate the studio or home, and they are non-flamable.

Comparison with Oil Paints. From the above list it is very easy to see the advantages of polymer emulsion over that of an oil medium. A comparative list follows.

1. Oil, when dry (after ten to twenty years), is a brittle film that will crack with expansion and contraction if rigid rules of application are not followed exactly.

2. Oil darkens and yellows with age and imparts its own yellowish-brown cast to a pigment.

3. The drying of oil is a slow, continuing chemical reaction of oxidation and polymerization, which eventually converts the oil to a solid "linoxyn." It takes three months for a normally thick first coat to dry enough for correct overpainting.

4. Because of the chemical nature of the drying process, chemical reaction of pigment can take place, changing the color.

5. Special rules must be followed for supports and for the correct grounding, priming, and sizing

of these supports, otherwise adhesion will be poor or the medium will deteriorate the support.

6. The rule of painting from "lean to fat" must be followed; a paint film containing a large percentage of oil should not be painted under a film containing a smaller percentage of oil, or cracking will result. This is further complicated by the fact that each oil color contains different percentages of oil in relation to pigment, and, in order to paint correctly, the artist must know the oil content of each color he uses. Slow drying, fatty paints will be sealed under the fast drying, lean paints; when the fatty paints underneath eventually dry, they will contract and crack the surface of the already dry outside lean paints.

7. Oils require three to six months drying time before a final varnish to protect the painting may be applied.

8. Oil has a lower resistance to ultra violet light than acrylics.

9. Turpentine, the solvent and thinner for oils, although not considered toxic in normal use, has a permeating odor, is inflammable, and can be irritating to certain people of allergenic inclination.

10. In one sense, the slow drying process is advantageous in that it permits prolonged blending of color. If artists today were accustomed to handling oil paints in the manner of the Old Masters, the slow drying time would be no handicap. But this is not the case; ours is an impatient age.

Toxicity. Because of misleading statements and misinformation over the past few years as to the toxicity of certain materials used by the artist, it should be made quite clear that polymer emulsions are nontoxic.

Most pigments used in polymer emulsions are not toxic, and this includes Cadmiums and Phthalocyanines. I have seen some toxic pigments used in a poor grade of polymer similar to poster paint, but the company that produced it went out of business, so far as I know. The artist should be able to identify toxic materials; the exact chemical name of the pigment should be printed on the paint container so he can do so. The chemical name (not just a proprietary brand name) should also be shown so that the artist can check the permanency of the pigment against permanency charts.

The artist does use some mildly toxic materials, however, and he should be very careful to follow the warnings printed on the containers. For example, the removers for polymer emulsions are toxic and are so labeled. Artists have used lacquers, vinyl resins that require strong aromatic solvents, various epoxy combinations, polyesters, urethanes, etc. These materials can be highly toxic and have impaired the health of artists—including the writer—who used them *incorrectly*. In fact, one of my primary reasons for exploring polymer emulsions was that of health—I was poisoned by toxic thinners, and as a result became highly sensitive to any solvents, including turpentine. In order to paint, I had to find a completely nontoxic medium. The polymer emulsions were the answer.

If there is any doubt as to the toxicity of a material used in the art trade, the artist can consult *The Journal of the American Medical Association,* Vol. 204, No. 13, June 24, 1968: "Potential Health Hazards of Materials Used by Artists and Sculptors." This article covers the subject comprehensively.

Briefly, if the artist uses a material not manufactured for the art trade, he should be critically aware of all the possibilities—the good as well as the bad. The artist must know the technical problems inherent in any material he uses or he may kill himself—not only esthetically, but literally.

2

Polymer Emulsion Materials and Their Uses

This section is an important one for the reader because it explains the numerous materials available for polymer emulsion painting and related techniques and, as such, is a "ready reference section" to be used with this book as a whole. After this chapter it will be assumed that the reader has some basic understanding of the materials mentioned and long explanations will be omitted.

There are many brands of polymer emulsion colors and media on the market today and they are packaged in every conceivable type of container, from two-ounce metal tubes and studio-size tubes to plastic tubes and all kinds of bottles. It would be impossible to evaluate brand names at this point of polymer emulsion development because new brands appear on the market with regularity and also because those companies that have produced polymer emulsions for many years constantly change formulas to improve their product. Therefore, the following explanations are generalized to conform to most materials sold to the artist. Because it is reasonable to assume that there are good as well as bad quality polymer emulsions just as there are good and bad brands of oil paint, the artist should select and test his materials with care.

General Characteristics. In handling polymer emulsions there are no rules to follow as to paint application—almost anything can be done with relative permanency. Some rules do apply to painting supports and these are detailed in Chapter 3. Most of the time the artist can be as free as his inclination or imagination suggests.

Polymer emulsions are, as the term indicates, water soluble paints when in their liquid state. They can be mixed or thinned with water, and

cleaned from the palette and brush with water, while they are still wet. If too much water is added the binder of the paint (which is polymer resin) will be washed out or too far diluted to form a permanent film. Therefore, it is a good practice to add half polymer medium and half water, not just water alone, if maximum permanency is desired. Exceptions to this suggestion are treated specifically in later chapters.

Overpainting can be initiated as soon as the paint is dry to the touch. This is true even in thick applications. *Alla prima* techniques can continue for hours if the paint is kept in its wet state by working the whole painting at one time—as paint is added so is the water within the paint, thus keeping the surface wet. It is not recommended that multiple sprays of water be applied to the surface. This can also wash out the binder, if overdone, and then the surface film will not be waterproof.

When polymer emulsion paints and mediums dry they are waterproof and relatively permanent. They should not be allowed to dry in the brush or on any surface one does not want permanently painted. Keep brushes wet in a pail of water at all times. Do not allow polymer paint to dry on clothing as it makes a good textile paint and is difficult, if not impossible, to remove. Each company produces a remover for its product, which will dissolve the polymer when dry. These are very efficient removers—not only will they remove the paint but also, at times, the color from clothes and the bristles from the brush. Wear smocks or painting clothes. If polymer paints dry on clothing, perhaps the best thing to do is paint your clothing the same color as the dried splotch or work a design around the spatter.

Tubed Polymer Emulsion Colors. The difference between polymer emulsion paints in tubes and those in jars is mainly one of consistency—viscosity. The tubed color should have a thick body similar to that of oil paints. Although tubed polymer emulsions can give the visual effects and the surface quality of oil paints, if that is what the artist wishes, it will be quite evident with the first brush stroke that this is where the similarity ends. Tubed polymers will not have the *exact* same "feel" or the "push and pull" characteristic of oils, although today they are similar. They should hold crisp brush strokes and retain painting knife configurations. They will flow much more freely than oils, yet impastos can be applied without appreciable shrinkage.

If these qualities are not observed in the paint used then the artist should try another brand, if he expects to achieve an oil-like surface. Some brands are too thin, similar to the jar color or tempera consistency. Some are too thick and handle like liquid rubber, are gummy, and dry from the top down leaving skins that may be pulled around if painting continues for a long period of time.

Tubed polymer colors dry very fast, if compared to oil colors, but they dry much more slowly than polymer emulsion jar colors. In normal thicknesses of color, the tubed paints dry within thirty minutes to one hour. If thinned with water they dry in approximately fifteen minutes. If applied in impasto they will sometimes take several hours or overnight to dry thoroughly. Drying time, then, depends on how thickly the paint is applied. Drying is also affected by humidity, since polymers dry by water evaporation. The absorbency of the surface support will affect the drying time as well; a very absorbent surface cuts the normal drying time in half.

Blendings of color can be accomplished easily with tubed polymer emulsions if the artist works quickly and surely. The paints can be mixed on the palette and, if kept in small piles, can be worked for almost a full day. If a skin forms over the paint on the palette it can be lifted off and the paint underneath will still be soft enough to

use, if it has not dried overnight. It is not recommended that polymer emulsion colors be squeezed out onto the palette in advance in the usual oil arrangements. The colors to be mixed should be taken from the tube only as needed, enough to form small piles. Trying to save paint by squeezing out only a small dab at a time will waste paint instead, because it will dry too rapidly.

Tube colors produced in roll-up metal tubes do not dry out in the tube even if the cap is not replaced. In testing without a cap over a two-month period, the paint dried in the neck of the tube down about one revolution of the cap (approximately one-sixteenth of an inch). The dried paint acts as a sealer for the tube and can be easily removed with the tip of a painting knife or a nail; the remaining paint will be as workable as a new tube of color. Open paint tubes can be arranged on a large palette for ready use, eliminating both the necessity of wet paint palette arrangements and the bothersome intermediary step of constantly opening tubes for mixing. Polymer emulsion colors sold in plastic tubes do not work this way however: the plastic will suck air back into the tube, causing drying.

Most tube colors dry to a slight sheen, something like oil paints that have been slightly diluted with turpentine. The more transparent pigments have a somewhat higher gloss due to the ratio of pigment to binder. If a high gloss or completely matte surface is desired the different polymer mediums can be applied as a final varnish to the painting or they can be mixed with the colors directly. (See below.)

Tubed colors that harden in the tube, that separate in the tube (fluid medium or water and thick color being extruded at the same time), or that are gummy, grainy, gelatinous, glutenous, or are otherwise hard to manipulate are misformulations and should be returned to the manufacturer for replacement. Sometimes this is not the manufacturer's fault; the paints may have been left on a loading dock somewhere and gone through multiple freeze-thaw cycles, which some formulations cannot take. But in most cases it is the fault of the manufacturer. If the artist consistently finds such aberrations he should try another brand.

Because tubed colors are easy to transport and store and can be readily diluted with water and medium to the jar color or watercolor consistency, they are many times preferred by schools and students who have to make a choice. Those artists who want the look of oils, who want an impasto material, who like to work in painting knife techniques, who want to paint in "the manner of the Old Masters," or who prefer the Impressionist, Expressionist, or Spanish school of textural painting would do best with tubed polymer emulsion colors. (See Figure 1.)

Jar Polymer Emulsion Colors. The viscosity of polymer emulsion colors packaged in jars is usually between that of tempera paint or casein depending on the brand chosen. They adapt themselves to broad areas of flat brilliant color, and for this reason are used by the Hard Edge, Op, Minimal, and Pop painters of today. They are also readily adaptable to the Magic Realist school and many types of commercial design and illustration because they handle in the manner of tempera or egg tempera, or illustrators colors. The exact duplication of egg tempera, with none of its traditional inherent drawbacks, can be achieved by mixing the yolk of an egg with jar colors. That is, they can be painted on canvas, or paper, or any flexible support, in impasto if desired, without cracking or peeling in the normal expansion and contraction of the support, and the support can be rolled without problems.

Jar colors are especially good for polymer watercolor effects because they are more easily diluted with water than the tube colors and require less water to obtain watercolor consistency, thus producing more color strength and brilliancy.

The drying time of jar colors is very rapid, like that of tempera. They dry in about fifteen to twenty minutes and they dry waterproof. No blendings of colors can be achieved or mistakes be scrubbed out once the paint is dry. However, one great advantage of a fast-drying medium is that instead

Figure 1. This shows direct working possibilities with tube polymers, using brush and knife. Paint was squeezed onto the canvas from the tube and work proceeded immediately.

of making mud trying to correct a mistake, the mistake can be painted out within twenty minutes or less, depending on the thickness of the paint and the absorbency of the support. In fact, the whole painting can be repainted every fifteen minutes or so. Or, in a day's working time, the painter can do fifteen to thirty paintings, one on top of the other. This makes it possible to learn good technique rapidly and the painter can quickly change the form of the work as his concepts and reactions change.

Very little separation of pigment from medium occurs with a well-formulated jar color, but if a milky liquid should appear on top of the color, it is merely the emulsion binder and should be stirred in.

The jars give the artist wide-mouthed containers into which he can dip the brush directly. Since the jar color dries so quickly, it is better to work in this manner than to place jar color on the palette. Brushes can be dipped from jar to jar without muddying colors, for in most brands the paint is viscous enough to stick to the brush instead of dripping off into the jar. If a color does inadvertently drip off, it will stay on top of the color in the jar—not mix in and discolor—and can be easily lifted off with a dry brush. Thus colors stay clean even when dipping from jar to jar with a "dirty" brush.

Polymer emulsion colors dry very slowly in the jars, even with the caps off, because less surface is exposed to air than with paint placed on the palette, therefore less evaporation of water occurs. If the colors do begin to dry in the jar, they dry from the top down and the artist need only lift off the skin of paint that forms. The rest of the paint will be in perfect condition. However, the painter should be careful that paint skins are not mixed into the paint.

Some painters place a few drops of water on top of the color to prevent drying, but this is not recommended as a *constant* practice—the binder may become overly diluted and then the paint will not be permanent. This practice can also cause mold to form by altering the ratio of the mold-preventing agent, usually incorporated into polymer emulsion formulations. If water is added to prevent drying in the jar, or if a thick body is made more workable by the addition of water, then medium, as well as water, should be added in a half-and-half mixture. When jars are stored for a long period, half water and half medium should be poured *on top* of the color—not mixed in—to the depth of about a sixteenth of an inch.

The rims of jars must be wiped free of paint after use or the top will become solidly bonded to the jar. If the top does stick, hot water run over it for about a minute will release it with little trouble. Polymers are thermoplastic resins; the warmer they become, the more pliable they become.

One facet of jar polymer emulsion that seems to bother artists at times is that most jar colors have a relatively matte finish when dry. This, of course, as with tempera or casein, will diminish

the brilliancy of the color, and the evaporation of the water will cause a "color change." Some artists prefer this quality, others do not. The color does not "change" that much but brilliancy is diminished because in its wet state the paint has a higher rate of light reflection. If the artist prefers this gloss brilliance of wet colors he can restore approximately the original wet surface quality by giving the painting a coat of gloss medium, when dry. The painter will adjust to this factor quickly and his mind will almost automatically make the necessary compensations as to terminal results.

Illustrator Color. Some companies produce what they term "illustrator color." This is basically the same as jar color. In testing, these colors seem to be somewhat more dilute, with less body than most jar colors. Too often they tend to separate, water on top and color on the bottom, and require constant mixing to achieve proper consistency.

Gloss Medium. Mediums of various kinds are not a requirement in polymer painting. You can just use water and paint. However, to explore all the multiple possibilities of polymers, especially when applying polymer emusions in an oil technique, these mediums are necessary. (See Figure 2.)

Gloss medium is the basic medium produced. It is a milky-looking liquid with the consistency of light cream. Although milky when wet, it dries to a crystal clear, flexible film. The counterparts of gloss medium in oil painting are turpentine, linseed oil, damar varnish, copal medium, and everything else employed as varnish, thinner, or as mixing medium with oil paints.

The more gloss medium added to jar or tube colors the more fluid and the more transparent they become. Colors diluted greatly with gloss medium and applied with a red sable oil brush give smooth, beautifully brilliant, high gloss glazes. These polymer emulsion glazes can be much more intense and have a greater clarity than oil glazes. They will dry in fifteen to thirty minutes and overglazing can proceed as soon as they are dry to the touch. Twenty to thirty glazes with polymer emul-

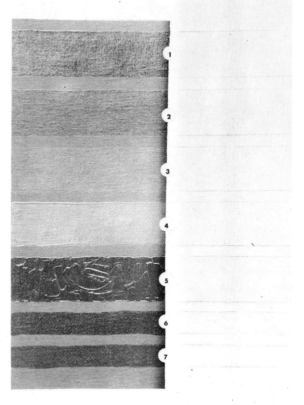

Figure 2. Polymer mediums can change the surface quality and the intensity of polymer colors. All mediums in this illustration were applied over black (at left) and extended out over the gesso ground. No. 1 is a gloss medium, which makes black appear darker and more intense as well as producing an oil-like gloss. No. 2 is matte varnish. This changes the color only slightly with a low, non-reflective sheen. No. 3 is matte medium, which will cloud dark colors if applied too heavily, as seen in No. 4, which is two coats of matte medium. No. 5 is gel in low impasto. It gives a high gloss and unusual effects. No. 6 shows SOLUVAR gloss varnish and No. 7 is SOLUVAR matte varnish. Both change the surface character of the paint, but No. 7 causes no gloss glare as does SOLUVAR gloss, which is more like a damar varnish in appearance.

sions can be accomplished in a day's time. If done in oils it would take over a year for the same results, if the proper drying time for oil paint glazes were observed.

Gloss medium is applied as a final varnish much in the same manner as is damar varnish with oils. (See Chapter 3, *Varnishing.*)

The addition of medium increases the adhesion of colors and makes them more lasting as well as imparting greater flexibility to the dry paint film. For maximum relative permanency the medium should be used with colors or used as a final varnish over the colors. When additives of raw pigment, textural materials, etc., are mixed with polymer emulsion colors, medium should always be added as well to keep the ratio of pigment to binder constant. If this is not done the paint may crack. The more absorbent the additive used, the more medium should be added. It is best to make a workable paste of medium and additive (about the viscosity of tube color) before mixing the materials into the paint.

If the gloss medium has too high a surface sheen for the artist's preference, matte varnish can be used or matte medium can be mixed with gloss medium to produce any degree of surface characteristics from high gloss to matte.

Care must be taken when the medium, or medium-diluted paint, is brushed over the painting surface—especially if the surface is textured or in any way in relief. If brushing is too vigorous in these cases, bubbles may form and they will dry permanently onto the surface. If the bubbles are quite small they will sometimes cause a milky look. When bubbles are observed, wipe them off immediately with a dry rag or dry brush. Of course if the artist likes permanent bubbles, he can achieve them. At one time there was a rash of "bubble paintings" in New York.

Matte Medium. As its name indicates, matte medium dries to a flat, dull, matte film. It is mixed with polymer emulsion colors to produce a matte surface with no reflection sheen. Because of this it decreases the visual intensity of the color. For maximum development of color intensity, do not use matte medium. (See Figure 2.)

Many companies produce only a matte medium. Others manufacture a matte varnish as well. When only matte medium is offered it is usually not as flat as the matte medium produced by companies that produce both. There is a reason for this somewhat confusing situation.

All basic polymer emulsion mediums are glossy. To make the medium matte, material has to be added to the medium to diffuse the light. Usually the additive is Collodial Silica (or some inert, semi-transparent pigment) or hard wax. These materials are only semi-transparent in nature. If too much is incorporated as a flatting agent they show up as a foggy or milky film when the matte medium is painted over the colors.

Companies that produce only a matte medium add less matting agent so that the matte medium can be used as a varnish as well as a mixing medium. This reduces the danger of clouding the colors when applied as a varnish. It also follows that this type of matte medium will not be completely matte, because less flatting agents are used. In reality it is a semi-matte medium.

Companies that offer both matte medium and matte varnish combine enough flatting materials to make the matte medium completely "dead" matte. This type of matte medium should be used only as a mixing medium—mixed with colors

only. **DO NOT** apply it as a final varnish, or the medium may fog the color. This is especially true if the color is dark. Actually, until the artist has a detailed knowledge of the medium he uses and all its characteristics, this is a good rule to follow with all types of matte medium. If this rule is not adhered to, the artist will find himself repainting the whole painting. Once matte medium has clouded a surface there is little that can be done. Some artists have used matte medium as a final varnish but only after extensive work and testing of the material.

Matte medium is one of the most adhesive of the polymer mediums and makes the best collage "glue." It is also an excellent priming material or sealer for absorbent surfaces. I personally prefer it to polymer gesso, although most painters will option for a white ground.

Matte Varnish. When a matte varnish is available in a polymer emulsion line, it is used, very simply, as a final varnish by those artists who do not like a high gloss finish. It is not as flat as the matte medium, having a low sheen something like that of encaustic. The explanation is that matte varnish is diffused with a hard wax at times. Although there is a slight sheen there is no glare or reflection to distort the paint surface. (See Figure 2.)

Give one final coat only. If heavy films or too many coats of matte varnish are used, the matte varnish, also, may show some clouding of color. Matte varnish can be mixed with polymer emulsion colors as well as applied as a varnish.

Resoluble Polymer Varnish. Relatively new to the market, a removable polymer varnish offers many advantages to artists as well as to museums. This varnish is a pure acrylic spirit formulation using mineral spirits (naphtha) as the remover. It is produced in gloss and matte finishes, which can be mixed in any proportions for the desired surface sheen. A coating of the standard polymer emulsion gloss medium is applied and allowed to dry overnight; then the resoluble (removable) varnish is brushed on in the same manner as a damar varnish would be brushed on for oil paintings. (See Figure 2.)

If dirt does accumulate on the surface the varnish is removed with mineral spirits or turpentine, taking the dirt with it. The painting is then revarnished.

Just as important an advantage is the ability of the resoluble varnish to reduce the pressure sensitivity, or "surface tack," from polymer emulsion paints, since all emulsion polymers are troubled with pressure sensitivity (some brands more than others), especially in hot weather.

(Refer to the **Glossary of Materials** for purchase information.)

Polymer Spray Varnish. There are many brands of "acrylic," "polymer," and "plastic" spray coatings on the market. Very few of these are suitable for polymer emulsion paints because of their high solvent content. The artist should take extreme precautions in using most of these. If the label does not indicate that the varnish is formulated for application over polymer emulsions or acrylic resins, do not use it or the painting may be ruined.

The polymer spray varnish is usually a pure acrylic resin dissolved in a volatile solvent and is a somewhat harder type of acrylic than is used for painting. Because of this a thin coating should be applied. If too heavy a buildup is given, the varnish surface may become brittle.

The spray varnish is used to adjust **surface sheen** (it is manufactured in gloss and matte) and *especially to reduce the pressure sensitivity of emulsion polymers.* It is a great asset in classes where works executed with polymer are stacked one on top of another.

Gel Medium. Gels were first produced to give a thick, oil-like body to jar colors. Gel is the same thing as polymer gloss medium only it has been thickened with resins and/or thickening agents. It dries clear in thin applications and produces a high gloss. If heavy impastos of over a sixteenth of an inch are applied at one time the gel may remain milky. (See Figure 2.)

Gel medium is an outstanding glue for heavy painting additives and can be used with the addition of a slight amount of color for unusual transparent-translucent impastos or textured glazes. It should hold brush and painting knife textures. (See Figure 3.)

Gel medium is an excellent mixing medium for raw pigments when the artist wishes to make his own colors. It can also extend the working time of emulsion colors, to a limited degree. The more gel used, the more transparent the color will become, the longer the working time, and the higher the gloss. (See Figure 5, Chapter 3.)

Polymer Gesso. Polymer gesso is similar in use to traditional gesso. It is a thick, brilliantly white liquid for sizing and grounding supports. Unlike traditional gesso, which is basically chalk or some other inert white bound with a gelatin or casein glue, polymer gesso is very flexible and can be used on flexible supports. It can be painted on canvas and the canvas can be rolled.

Polymer gesso dries very quickly, usually within thirty minutes depending on how thickly it is applied. Overpainting can proceed as soon as the surface is dry to the touch, thus eliminating the long waiting time after preparing traditional grounds.

The synthetic gessos may be used as grounds not only for the emulsion paints, but are excellent for use with oils, watercolors, tempera, encaustic, and even make ideal surfaces for silverpoint drawing.

It is not necessary that a ground be used for polymer painting; the paint itself acts as a sealer and protective coating for the support. Time and money can be saved by this omission. But there are reasons for grounding a support. First, most artists like a white or tinted ground. Second, the gesso, with its highly brilliant, non-yellowing and intense white, allows outstanding transparent glazes and washes. Indeed, a white ground is mandatory when glazes and washes are applied to achieve the reflection necessary for vivid color. Third, if the

Figure 3. When using textural materials, such as the gravel shown here, a generous amount of gel medium should be mixed in with the paint and the additive to create a permanent and flexible painting material.

support is porous then the gesso is used to seal the surface so expensive colors will not be brushed into or soaked up by the support. Fourth, the polymer gesso usually has a slight tooth, or roughness, which can give better drag and control to the brush stroke.

Synthetic gesso may be applied in one or more coats, depending on the surface quality desired. It can be sprayed, brushed, or rolled on with a felt "house paint" roller. A very even smooth coating is achieved when gesso is diluted with about fifteen to thirty per cent water and brushed on in three or more applications. Each coat should be applied at right angles to the preceding coat to minimize brush strokes. If gesso is diluted over twenty per cent with water, the water should be mixed with one-third medium (matte or gloss) to insure the permanency of the gesso. Succeeding coats can be sanded with wet carborundum sandpaper of a very fine tooth to produce an outstandingly beautiful smooth ground.

Many types of textural effects can be accomplished by incorporating inert additives with the gesso. Grounds of this sort should be used on rigid panels. Each additive should be completely soaked in a polymer medium before mixing with the gesso, to produce maximum flexibility.

Modeling Paste. There are two basic types of polymer modeling pastes the artist can purchase. One is said to be flexible, the other is non-flexible.

Modeling paste is primarily marble dust and polymer medium with other materials added to achieve whiteness, tooth, etc. If the paste is supposedly flexible a large percentage of gel or medium is incorporated in manufacturing. An inflexible paste is heavily loaded with marble dust. The artist can make a rigid-set paste "flexible" by adding gel medium, half by volume.

The reason for the qualifications above in referring to "flexible" modeling paste is that, in testing, the supposedly "flexible" pastes prove only marginally so and will usually crack if a flexible support is used and the support is rolled, bent, or handled with anything but extreme care.

Flexible pastes are employed for textural painting and impastos only and, like all types of polymer pastes, should be applied to rigid supports such as hard board to insure that cracking will not occur later. They are not appreciably opaque and are slightly heavier in body than the tube colors. Non-flexible paste is a very stiff white or cream-colored putty used to build three-dimensional forms, sculpture, and to produce impastos or, with the addition of gel, for painting techniques in the manner of their more flexible counterparts.

Single layers of modeling paste as it comes from the container should be no more than one-quarter inch thick. If piled too heavily the paste tends to dry too fast and cause shrinkage cracks. If a greater thickness is desired, succeeding layers can be added to any depth. To save time, a heavy area can be applied and when cracks develop on drying they can be filled in with more paste. Modeling paste achieves a molecular bond with itself; areas can be added at any time—even ten years later—and the artist is assured the bond is durable.

For sculptural purposes, modeling paste should be handled in the same manner as clay. It should be cured—dried slowly—in a slightly open plastic bag. In a few days, depending on humidity and the mass being cured, the paste will go to the consistency of modeling clay and can be handled in the same manner of direct modeling as clay. All the same rules will apply: the hands should be kept slightly damp to prevent rapid water evaporation and the paste is draped with a damp cloth or sealed in a plastic bag to keep the exact state of malleability desired. In several more days of curing the paste will achieve the consistency of soap and can easily be carved. Approximately a week of curing will produce a hard, completely stable piece of stone more durable than concrete and practically impervious to weathering.

Modeling paste cannot be cast. Solid castings in a mold cannot be made because the form must be open to the air so water can evaporate from the paste.

Dry modeling paste will expand and contract through freeze-thaw cycles without cracking. It can be textured and colored to look like wood or any type of stone or can be polished to a marble sheen with a fine carborundum sandpaper that has been soaked in water. It is used for frame decorations, bas relief, sculpture repair, and massive sculptural forms. It can be used in solid mass or built in layers over a solid core of styrofoam, wood, papier mâché, etc.

Retarder. Although there are a few retarders available to lengthen the working time of polymer emulsion paints, I would suggest that the artist avoid them if he possibly can. Retarders are like fast drying siccatives (Japan or Cobalt driers) used with oil paints: they violate the nature of the materials used. If the artist wants to paint slowly he can use oils. If he wants to use polymers he should speed up his working processes.

Some retarders I have tried seem to incorporate oils or glycerin to inhibit water evaporation and these should be shunned as they may prevent the correct film-forming characteristics of polymer emulsions. If a retarder seems necessary, certain types of glycols can be employed with relative safety. The artist should try to obtain a retarder identified as such. If this is not possible, Propylene Glycol can usually be obtained through a local druggist. Propylene Glycol is an inexpensive chemical with the viscosity of glycerin. It should be used with restraint, however. Add only enough to do the job. This will take a bit of experimentation on the part of the artist; only a few drops should be added at a time until the artist is familiar with the drying time of his mixtures in relation to the thickness of paint applied. If too much glycol is added skins will form on top of the paint, which can easily be pulled down into fresh paint if painting continues for any appreciable working span.

Glycols can be of some advantage when polymer emulsion paints are used as a silk-screen ink in large screens.

Glycerine should not be used as a retarder. It will never dry, is volatile, and attracts moisture.

Polymer Remover. Almost every company that produces a polymer emulsion paint also packages a solvent that will remove its product. For acrylics the remover is a high volatile solvent such as lacquer thinner, xylol, or tuluol. These materials are flammable and the vapors can be toxic. They are so labelled and should be used according to directions.

The remover for most vinyls or for most polymer emulsions containing a high vinyl percentage is denatured alcohol.

3

General Information on Processes and Related Materials

Supports. Polymer emulsion media require few rules to hamper the artist's expressive range but there is one rule to which the artist must adhere at all times if he expects permanency. It has to do with painting supports: do not paint on an oily, greasy, or hard shiny surface.

Do not paint on any oily surface such as correctly primed oil canvas, oily or resinous woods, or *over oil paint.* Do not paint on a greasy surface that includes hand or finger print marks on the surface. Do not paint over an impervious, non-porous, or shiny surface such as glass, metal, Formica, waxed surfaces, or hardboards. Hardboard, fiberboard, or pressed panels can be used if the shine is removed with sandpaper.

Polymer emulsion media (including gesso and mediums as well as colors) will stick to all of these surfaces initially, but if water is applied there is a good chance that the polymer will release, peel off, or bubble. Since the recommended cleaning procedure is to wash with soap and water, it would be impossible to clean the painting without ruining it.

The average (poor) oil-primed canvases manufactured for the artist have a sufficiently low quantity of oil so that the water-base paints can form a bond to them, but they are not highly recommended. Raw canvas is best. Many companies produce polymer-primed canvas now and these are excellent. Since polymer is a good ground

for oils, in the near future most canvas will be polymer-primed. Other cloth supports recommended are burlap, linen, cotton, cheese cloth applied to board with polymer medium, sail cloth, and some synthetic fabrics. Synthetics should first be tested as to compatibility. If a cloth is sized by the manufacturer, then the sizing should be removed by washing the cloth in warm water before painting.

There is a simple test for checking the compatibility of any surface for polymer painting. Paint on a spot of color and let it dry thoroughly—overnight is best. Then take a wet sponge and dampen the dried paint. When the paint is quite damp (wait a couple of minutes to be sure) push at the paint film with your thumb. If the paint does not release from the surface, the support is a good one.

Other supports for use with polymer emulsions include sanded hardboard, either tempered or untempered; papers of all types; chipboard; matte board; illustration board; cardboard; masonry surfaces; and certain types of clear plastic sheets.

Synthetic paints actually protect the support as opposed to the deteriorative effects caused by oils. Thus a sizing is not necessary, as it is with oil paint, in order to prevent the oil medium from attacking and destroying the support. In fact a glue-sized canvas should never be used as a polymer ground —it will strip off cleanly when polymer is applied.

Grounds such as polymer gesso or matte medium may be used in order to gain a special surface quality or seal porous surfaces. Highly porous or absorbent surfaces should be given a priming so that the water will not be absorbed from the paints before coherent films form.

The polymer emulsions produce the most flexible paint film available today. A canvas can be rolled as soon as the paint is dry—sometimes within ten minutes after the last brush stroke has been applied. For transportation, meeting deadlines, and storage purposes this is very advantageous.

Metals or non-porous and smooth surfaces can be painted with polymer emulsion paints if the surface can be given a slight tooth. This can be achieved with abrasive action using carborundum papers or sand blasting. Many artists today use aluminum as a support, and this can be etched with acids. A lye (sodium hydroxide) solution will work. A five-per-cent solution of sodium hydroxide will etch the surface in about four minutes. The surface is flushed with water from a hose to stop the action. A weaker solution may prove less hazardous but, of course, take longer. Several minutes after the bubbling action on the surface begins will be enough time to provide a tooth for the paints. The area for preparing the surface should be resistant to lye and water, a concrete floor or open ground being best. The worker should be protected with rubber on feet and hands when using lye.

When heavy impasto is applied, especially if aggregates are used to a great extent, a rigid support is needed because of a decrease in flexibility of the entire paint film. Masonite is probably the best and most available rigid surface. Don't make a major project out of it, but do remember to remove the shine with sandpaper.

If a texture is desired as well as a rigid support, canvas or cloth can be applied to almost any surface from Masonite to masonry walls. This is done by cementing the material to the support with polymer gel medium. The backing should first be smoothed because any under-roughness or texture will show as bumps, lines, or uneven areas on the final surface. Before mounting fabric, the support should be given a coat of gesso or matte medium to seal the surface so it will not absorb water from the gel and make it set so fast it cannot be handled.

Polymer gel medium is employed as a cement because it will not dry as quickly as fluid mediums and because it has a high viscosity that will hold a fair amount of weight. Gel can be applied with a brush, painting knife, or, for large areas, with an adhesive cementing trowel that has a serrated edge. If the area is large it should be worked in sections. Starting at the top, trowel on gel, apply the fabric and roll it flat with a brayer or rubber roller. It is difficult to say how much gel to apply —it depends on the weight and texture of the material. An excess amount should be avoided as it will cause lumps if not completely worked out from under the edges. Light fabrics will stick to the surface without problems; heavy materials should be taped at the top until dry. Allow several days for thorough drying and the support is ready for painting. This process provides a completely homogenous sealer, adhesive, ground, and paint— all being polymer emulsions.

The above brief list of supports and processes only begins to suggest the diverse possibilities. Others will be outlined in later chapters dealing with specific techniques.

Palettes. Polymer emulsion media does not adhere to oily, greasy, or hard shiny surfaces. Therefore, these surfaces make the best palettes because dried films can be easily stripped from the surface with water. No thinners or removers are necessary —only water. (See Figure 4.)

A Formica-top table makes a good palette, but the best is probably opaque white glass of one-quarter-inch thickness. Its whiteness allows the artist to mix and see true tones and tints. White plastic firmly attached with waterproof tape under a clear glass will make a fair substitute. The edges must be sealed to keep water and paint from running under the edges.

Figure 4. A glass palette allows dried polymer to be soaked with water and stripped from the surface as plastic skins. Not only is this an easy cleaning procedure but the skins of paint can be used as collage material.

For those who find that polymer emulsion colors dry too fast on the palette, a white enamel tray with a high edge is recommended. Butcher's trays of this sort are sold as watercolor palettes in art stores, and one of the best is a photographer's wash tray. Paint can be kept for days in a workable state on these trays if a sheet of self-adhering plastic wrap is stretched over the top to seal in the moisture. If desired, the paint can be saved for weeks in this manner by placing a wet sponge in the center of the tray to increase the air moisture. Plastic ice trays or egg trays will also work if large areas are not needed for mixing colors.

The majority of paper throw-away palettes for oil painting should be avoided. Water media will buckle them like a wash board and paint will run off the sides. Furthermore, they have a hole cut through the paper to resemble the romantic notion of an "Old Master's" palette, evidently so the painter can walk around with his thumb stuck through the hole posing as an "artist." All this does is allow the paint to seep down the hole, cementing the paper together and defeating the purpose of the rip-off disposable palette. There are some sensible paper palettes, without the hole, made of a coated paper suitable for water-based paints as well as oil. They usually are identified as "polymer" or "acrylic" palettes.

Colors should not constantly be mixed over dry paint on the palette. This will release the dried polymer films and these skins become mixed with the fresh colors, ruining them.

Modeling paste is a very strong adhesive, as is matte medium. If modeling paste is allowed to dry on a hard shiny surface over a few days it will sometimes be so difficult to remove that the glass or enamel will chip. The paste is not porous enough for water to seep through the film and lift it. Since the palette is so quickly and easily cleaned—a damp cloth will take off wet color—it is not much bother to keep the palette free of polymer materials and mixtures and free of problems.

Brushes. All types of artists' brushes, watercolor as well as oil, may be used with polymer emulsions. Buy either a good grade, expensive brush or the cheapest. Good brushes can be cleaned with polymer remover; the bristles are well set in the ferrules. In an in-between price range, remover will not only take out the dried paint but may take the bristles out of the brush as well. Cheap brushes can be thrown away without too much loss. But good brushes produce better work with less trouble.

Do not allow polymer paints to dry in the brush. Usually, if you do, you will wind up with a solid plastic brush. And there is little you can do with a solid plastic brush—except maybe exhibit it as sculpture, these days. Keep dirty brushes in water, bristles down. This is probably contrary to all that has been said about the care of brushes, but with polymers it is best to do this rather than allow paint to dry in the brush if it cannot be cleaned immediately. Again, a good bristle brush can take this sort of treatment. Pure and very expensive red sable brushes cannot, however. They should be immediately cleaned and shaped after use.

If polymer does dry on a brush, wash it in *hot* water and soap. This will loosen the paint and it can be worked out—but not without some difficulty and time.

Polymer brushes are on the market and some of them are excellent. They have a nylon-type bristle, which is a hard shiny surface. Polymer emulsions will not stick, and if they dry in the brush can easily be washed out with warm water and soap. Nylon brushes do not wear out as quickly as natural bristle and are less expensive. They cannot produce the effect of a red sable as yet, but they do a good job as a bristle. For classroom work they should be preferred.

Painting and Palette Knives. The same kinds of knives are used with polymer as with any other media. Do not allow them to stay wet or they will rust. Wipe off the paint and water after use.

Varnishing. A polymer emulsion painting does not necessarily require a final varnish. However, to provide a protective surface that will absorb physical wear, to protect thin glazes and especially watered-down paints, or to adjust the degree of surface gloss or matte to a desired level, a varnish may be applied in either gloss or matte finish.

There is another reason to apply varnish. When polymer colors dry there is a slight amount of pigment on the surface, which has not been completely bound into the plastic film. This is especially true when water has been used with the paint. A damp cloth rubbed across the surface with pressure will lift off a bit of color. It does not usually muddy or stain other areas of color, but it does show on a clean white cloth. This is normal and should not be of much concern, but to prevent it a coat of varnish is required. Varnishing may proceed as soon as the paint is dry—within a couple of hours, or with extreme impasto, overnight.

I would recommend the resoluble polymer varnish as the best final coating for a painting. Easily and safely removed with mineral spirits, even after many years, it keeps dirt from becoming imbedded in the paint surface and prevents the polymer from becoming highly pressure sensitive. Matte and gloss are available.

Before using the resoluble varnish first give the painting a full coat of *gloss* medium as described below. Allow this protective coating to dry overnight and then apply the final varnish—matte or gloss or a mixture of the two. The resoluble varnish can be thinned with mineral spirits by twenty-five per cent to obtain a smoother flow. Turpentine can also be employed, but nothing stronger. A resoluble polymer varnish will usually take a full day to dry completely even though it may be dry to the touch before that time. It can be cleaned with soap and water in the same manner as cleaning any polymer painting, if removal of the varnish is not required because of imbedded dirt. Once the resoluble varnish is removed, more can be applied to the dry surface. In other words, it lends itself to traditional cleaning, restoring, and re-varnishing.

The best method of varnishing a polymer painting is by spray gun. Bubbles are avoided, there are no brush strokes to mar the surface, and the coating is infinitely more uniform. There are a number of spray apparatuses available and the artist has to pick one that conforms to his needs. For small paintings and for the painter with more technique than money a pressure unit can be used. A very good little unit is the Sprayon Jet-Pak manufactured by Sprayon Products, Inc., of Cleveland, Ohio. Pressure is delivered from a non-toxic, non-flammable pressure can attached to a sprayer head. A mid-range unit with professional possibilities would be better and produce a finer, more controllable spray mist. The spray pressure should be between forty and sixty pounds. The Mistral Miniature by Tritech, Inc., is an example that produces pressure from an electrically powered oscillating pump as opposed to a pressure tank employed in very expensive, professional units. It is compact and easily transportable. Spray apparatus is available at house paint or hardware stores rather than art supply houses.

Mouth atomizers and Flit guns have been used, but are not the best.

Care must be taken in spray varnishing. Several fine mists should be applied. Do not spray on heavy coats of varnish. They will run and ruin the painting. Test the action of the spray before varnishing to be sure the spray is a fine mist, not large globules spurting onto the surface, forming beads of distortion.

Matte varnish or gloss medium must be thinned with water to obtain the correct spray action. Twenty to forty per cent is about average water dilution. The lower the percentage of water used to acquire the best spray mist the better. Use a quick back and forth motion of the unit, starting the swing off the painting and continuing the swing off the sides.

Polymer varnishes can also be applied with a brush. The brush should be of high quality, with soft hair, and specifically made for the purpose. It should be relatively thin so that not too much varnish will be deposited.

To achieve an even coat the medium should be slightly thinned with water. Varnishing must be accomplished as rapidly and smoothly as possible in continuous strokes from one side of the painting to the other, either vertically or horizontally, as the artist prefers. Over-exuberant brush work, however, will produce a froth of bubbles. If bub-bles do occur, they can be removed by wiping a completely dry brush quickly over the area before it dries.

Varnish should not be restroked over partially dried varnish or the film will rub up at a critical drying point and the flake-like whitish particles produced will become bound into the painting. If at all possible use only one coat of varnish. For more gloss several coats can be applied but only after the first coat is completely dry.

The varnishes look milky immediately when applied over a painting, but they dry clear as glass within a few minutes, and create a brilliantly transparent film that will never yellow or change color.

A special varnishing technique used by *Syd Solomon* may be of interest to other artists. Solomon, who has worked with synthetics for years, mixes his own varnish for paintings. He shaves bees-wax into a double boiler, melts it, pours polymer medium into it, and warms the mixture. The proportion of wax medium is varied according to the degree of gloss desired; the more wax the less gloss. To varnish a painting he blows the warm mixture through a mouth atomizer onto the painting. He always varnishes outdoors on sunny days, because a sun-warmed painting seems to reduce the pull of the varnish against the paint and also helps avoid bubbles. Sometimes he uses a cheap Flit gun instead of a mouth atomizer; if so, he throws the gun away after use because it becomes clogged with dry varnish.

Mixing Pigments. It is possible for the artist to create his own polymer emulsion paints by mixing dry powdered pigment with polymer mediums. There are reasons both for doing this as well as reasons for not doing it.

Money can be saved by using less expensive pigments than those used by fine art companies. In the classroom a good powdered tempera can be employed for experimental work, but the pigments are not as permanent as artist-grade colors and will fade. Polymer mediums, in themselves, do

Figure 5. It is easier to mix powdered pigments with polymer when gel medium is used. The gel is squeezed from the tube in a round circle and the dry pigment is spooned into the center as seen in the top illustration. The gel is then folded over the pigment and mixed to a paste-like consistency. It is important to bring the under-mixture to the top with the palette knife as seen in the bottom photograph. The pigment used here was a red-orange fluorescent, a very light weight, fluffy material. It would have been very difficult to mix in a more fluid medium.

not keep a pigment from fading. What they do is screen out, in final varnishes, some of the ultra-violet light that causes fading and thus make the pigment somewhat more light-fast. But if the pigment fades, it will still fade despite the screening effect of the polymer and should not be used for professional work. Powdered tempera and medium will produce most of the handling characteristics of polymer.

Pigment has to be mixed with medium and used immediately. Do not mix a polymer paint and store it on the shelf. Many pigments react with the chemical nature of polymers and sometimes go bad in a matter of hours—or in a few minutes in some cases. Glutenous masses, rubbery junk, or solid blobs of polymer form quite readily. So mix the paint and apply it immediately. Once the paint has dried on the surface no reactions will

29

occur and the artist is safe. With this in mind, it is many times cheaper to buy manufactured paint than to mix it.

Sometimes the artist has no other choice than to mix his own paints because he needs a color other than those manufactured in a polymer line. This has been especially true in the optical school of painting when fluorescent paints were wanted.

In mixing pigments use gel medium as the binder. It is much easier to use than the more fluid matte and gloss mediums. Many pigments are very light-weight fluffy powders and if placed in a fluid medium tend to float on top of the medium. It can take hours to mix pigments of this nature—especially fluorescent pigments and transparent dye pigments such as Phthalocyanine blues and greens. Gel medium eliminates this problem.

Pile gel or squeeze it out onto the palette in a thick circle. Pour the pigment into the doughnut hole and, with a large painting knife that has a very wide blade, fold the gel over the pigment. Continue to fold and refold the mixture, making sure that the bottom gel is turned to the top. In a few minutes a paint results. It is the consistency of tube color and can be thinned with water to flowing body. (See Figure 5.)

There is a problem of how much pigment to add to the gel. Each pigment has its own requirement as to how much binder it needs to make a permanent, waterproof and flexible paint. To pre-check this before mixing a quantity of paint, paint a small amount of the mixed pigment that will be used onto a flexible support in a slight impasto. When it dries, wet a white cloth and wipe the surface. If no color comes off, the binder ratio is excellent. Then fold the support. If the paint does not crack it is usually flexible enough and the artist will have a pigment-binder ratio for that particular color from then on. Until the artist is familiar with the pigment-medium ratio on a "second-nature" basis, this process is a large bother. But it is necessary to prove durability.

Correct mixtures of the above sort will have a slight gloss due to the gel. If a matte surface is desired, mix in matte medium or cover with matte varnish when dry. A slight amount of water will also flat the gel paint enough at times.

Testing Polymer Emulsion Paints. Although we have much information spanning a period of almost twenty years, we still do not have "the test of time" to state emphatically that polymer emulsions are ten or twenty times more permanent than oil paints. To do this we would have to wait a period of two thousand years or so and most of us just do not have the time. So we have to depend on relatively reliable tests from the chemist, the laboratory, and painters. All information indicates the superior durability of polymers.

Fadeometer (arc light) tests, although not as true an indication as direct sunlight, show pigments fade less in polymer suspensions than in oil. Direct and highly controlled daylight exposure shows the durability of the polymer binders to be better than that of oil. Polymer emulsion house paints, in use for over fifteen years outdoors in all manner of applications, definitely attest to the superiority over oils. They have withstood the rigors of salt spray on houses and fine art murals as well as withstanding high humidity and excessive sun exposure for over ten years now and are still in good condition. An oil paint would have failed in much less time. The information is recorded and reliable. Since we assume the results and statements of modern chemistry to be correct almost every day of our lives, even to the point of life or death decisions, we should also allow that in the field of artists' paints they are probably correct as well.

There are rather simple controlled tests the artist, the professor, or the class can make to show how well vehicles will retain their elasticity, freedom from cracking and flaking, and pigment stability. If a person doubts the durability of a paint he can make his own judgements by following the procedures below. These tests should be made by the artist who mixes his own selection of pigments with medium.

A stretched canvas not less than sixteen by twenty inches should be used for the test. This will allow for a good amount of expansion and contraction of the canvas, which causes dried paint films to crack. The selected paint is applied to the canvas in thin to thick films, overpainting, and with impasto pilings. Impastos should predominate with no extra medium added. Such impastos are more prone to failure and therefore will show defects in binder much more quickly.

If the test is for comparison of different media, the same pigments should be used in each medium and applied in an identical manner on duplicate canvas.

If the test is done to check light-fastness of pigments suspended in a specific medium, then the bottom half of the test canvas is masked out with opaque black tape or paper securely attached to the canvas at all edges to block out any light.

To check either durability or light fastness, the test canvas is suspended inside a window facing south, just a few inches away from the glass. If the room is not too well heated the canvas will be subjected to both extremes of temperature and humidity. Southern exposure will allow enough sunlight to show film embrittlement. (For more professional results the canvas is placed in a sort of "hot-bed box," which has a single-thickness glass several inches from the paint surface. The sealed, glass-topped box should be placed at a forty-five degree angle to the vertical, facing south.)

Six months of exposure in the above tests will provide adequate results. Pigments should show relative fading or yellowing and paint films should become brittle, if they are going to, in this time. If no cracks develop, the thumb should be pushed along the back of the canvas under impastos to see if fine cracks will show or if any loss of adhesion to the support is evident.

Testing of compatible surfaces is described under *Supports,* in this chapter.

Cleaning. After a polymer emulsion painting dries, water will no longer affect it. Thus, soap and water are the recommended cleaning agents. Do not use harsh solvents to clean polymer paints, as is done with oil paints. Especially do not apply volatile solvents such as lacquer thinner, acetone, xylol, toluol, etc., as dirt removers. They will destroy the painting.

Some artists attach information sheets to the backs of all polymer emulsion paintings, stating the type of synthetic resin, the brand name, and cleaning procedures. It is a good practice to follow.

In cleaning with soap and water, the water should be cold or luke warm at most and should not be allowed to remain on the surface longer than necessary. All the soap should be removed. Although soap and water are preferred, I have used household abrasive cleaners in stubborn cases where grease and dirt from hands have soiled a work—especially in the case of unvarnished gesso, which picks up and holds dirt tenaciously.

To allow traditional cleaning of paintings by removal of a final varnish, use a resoluble polymer varnish as described under *Varnishing* in this chapter. It is highly recommended to avert many troubles in cleaning and restoration. If a resoluble varnish is used a note should be applied to the back of the painting stating this fact.

4

Suggested Outline for Media Exploration

The succeeding chapters are arranged according to broad technical approaches with polymer emulsions so that an outline form of media exploration can be followed. This is only a *suggested* approach for the classroom, or for individual independent study. Each artist or instructor will have his own direction and will, of course, give emphasis to various techniques in the outline suggestions.

Technical groupings and esthetic directions will vary from the traditional point of view because the inherent characteristics of polymer emulsions

TECHNIQUE APPROACH	PROBLEM	SUGGESTED DIRECTION
1. Watercolor, wet-in-wet fluid application.	Discover wet-in-wet possibilities and intense polymer coloration.	Informal application of intense color. Can work into paint-suggested subject or abstract form.
2. Watercolor, wet-in-wet fluid application with medium control.	To control flow of fluid techniques with polymer mediums.	Use atmospheric subject or design. Masses and linear edges controlled with gloss medium or matte varnish.
3. Transparent water-color. Traditional application.	Control of polymer to duplicate traditional effects.	Work from subject (model/still life). Line contrasted with wash. Main point: discover differences in intensity and mixing of colors as opposed to traditional w/c.
4. Polymer w/c approach using overwashes.	Discover effects of painting washes over dried polymer color.	a. Symmetrical and geometric design to explore formal color relationships possible with permanent w/c. b. Asymmetrical and free-form design using polymer wash over dry wash, line, and dry-brush. Atmospheric, intuitive color.
5. Opaque w/c, gouache.	Value of opaque effects, heavy color.	Work from transparent to opaque. Stress mass, volume of subject. Use heavy color possible with polymer.
6. Watercolor resist.	Explore effects of resist materials.	Combination of above effects with resist technique. Emphasis on continuity via diverse techniques.
7. Student choice of w/c (Optional).	Develop deeper under-standing of preferred polymer w/c approach.	Use any or all of above directions for personal expression. Stress design, composition, color.

will be followed and this will cut through the usual classifications. Since there are no valid lines today between sculpture and painting, realism and abstraction, the artist should be equally free in the areas of technical approach. Therefore the reader will find Hard-Edge Optical art in the same water-paint approach as traditional water-color or tempera renderings. Not only is this grouping more consistent technically and developmentally but it also allows for more esthetic freedom as well.

It is assumed that all elements of artistic expression—form, shape, color, design, line, etc.— will be of primary importance throughout the polymer explorations.

If the following outline is adhered to, more or less, the work will take at least a semester, or, if explored fully and expanded, a school year. Not only does it cover most of the techniques possible with polymer emulsions, and perhaps create new ones, but most esthetic developments from traditional to contemporary are indicated and these, too, can be expanded.

MEDIA	SUPPORT	REFERENCE
Jar color and water. Large sabeline wash brushes.	Heavy w/c paper and/or porous paper, rice paper.	Chapter 5 Figs. 6, 7.
Jar color and water. Large sabeline wash brushes, small, pointed w/c brush. Mediums.	Heavy w/c paper.	Chapter 5 Fig. 7.
Jar color and water. Large wash brushes, small w/c brushes.	Rough tooth, heavy w/c paper.	Chapter 5 Figs. 6, 7.
Jar color and water. Any w/c brushes.	Smooth surface, w/c paper. If wrinkles occur, wet and use weight to flatten surface.	Chapter 5
Jar color, water. Titanium White. Any w/c brushes.	Matte board, illustration board.	Chapter 5 Fig. 9.
Jar color, water, rubber cement, oil, crayon, masking tape, etc. Variety of w/c brushes.	Smooth or slightly toothed illus. board, w/c paper, synthetic papers.	Chapter 5 Figs. 8, 9.
Any mentioned above.	Student choice.	Chapter 5

TECHNIQUE APPROACH	PROBLEM	SUGGESTED DIRECTION
8. Direct tempera application.	To discover handling and control of undiluted jar color.	Abstract and/or expressionistic application. Work must be fast. Spatial push and pull through paint application and color. Immediate overpainting. OR Figurative approach stressing pattern and design, positive and negative space, flat color.
9. Tempera or egg tempera.	Achieve exact control in detail tempera buildup. Importance of polymer ground.	Work from detailed drawing of subject. Individual, brush stroke by brush stroke buildup from sketch. Take time, patience to achieve magic realist effect. May extend over several weeks working time while working concurrently with other techniques. Emphasize pictorial space modeling of forms in both fore- and rear-ground.
10. Loose tempera approach in control.	Achieve exact control of chance elements in spontaneous application, abstract detail.	Use detailed subject matter at painting focal point. Contrast with negative space developed to realistic approach through chance application of polymer. Re-establish gesso ground over areas which do not work. Work quickly in large negative areas.
11. Thick casein application.	Effect a heavy paint texture through tempera-casein approach.	Loose handling of polymer, with subject matter, to build a tactile surface in casein manner. Limited palette and subdued color. Dynamic composition activated with diagonals, etc. Departure from planar relationships.
12. Optical intensity in tempera application achieving hard edges through investigation of tape techniques.	Develop maximum intensity of color innate in polymers. Discover proper flow of paint and how to use tape for precise results. Realize what "paint fast" means.	Abstract, formal symmetry. Colors used purely in multi-application to discover depth and intensity of color change. Juxtaposition of color to achieve color vibrancy. Modular units can be used effectively. Tapes should be used for precise edges. Color relationships worked out previous to painting. Work VERY fast in color applications.
13. Optical intensity of polymer in masked free-form approach.	Same as above. Also how to achieve large, precise, impersonal areas of maximum intense color. Color relationships more intuitively perceived.	a. Asymmetrical, more personal design. Large areas of single color controlled through tape and paper masking. Control surface with FAST brush application. b. Pop imagery. Control of intense color with spray application and masking.

MEDIA	SUPPORT	REFERENCE
Jar color. One-quarter-to one-inch bristle brushes.	Heavy paper (all purpose). Paper board.	Chapter 5 Figs. 10, 11, 15.
a. Jar color plus slight amount of water and/or gloss medium OR b. Jar color plus medium and egg yolk. Small, red sable w/c brushes for most work.	Masonite panel with several coats of sanded gesso, OR gesso on illustration board.	Chapter 5 Figs. 12, 13, 14, 61, 62. Color Page 49.
Jar color, water mediums. Various brushes, rags, sponges, paper, etc.	Masonite panel with several coats of sanded gesso.	Chapter 5 Figs. 12, 13, 14, 58. Color Page 49.
Thick jar color with inert clay if necessary, OR water-thinned tube color. Large bristle brushes. Palette mixing.	Large, heavy paper, or paper board, or cardboard, not under 2 x 3 feet.	Chapter 5
Jar color thinned with water and/or slight amount of medium. Medium to isolate color applications. Soft brushes or nylon brushes, VERY large.	Raw cotton duck primed with 3 coats gesso. Seal with medium. Canvas size not under 3 x 3 feet, preferably larger, to produce impact of color.	Chapter 5, Tapes, Stripping of Tapes Figs. 16, 17, 19. Color Page 52.
Jar color thinned with water and/or medium. a. soft brushes. b. spray unit.	Raw cotton primed with 3 coats of gesso. Seal with medium. Large canvas, not under 3 x 3 feet.	Chapter 5, Sprays, Tapes Figs. 20,21,22,24,25,27. Color Pages 61, 64.

TECHNIQUE APPROACH	PROBLEM	SUGGESTED DIRECTION
14. Staining.	Control-intense stains of polymer. Make color "float."	Abstract application of thin color on raw surface. Atmospheric illusionism. Background and foreground should merge. Control flow with horizontal canvas. Tilt or tie to obtain shapes and intensities. Pour on color.
15. Combination of staining with related techniques.	To determine if purity of color field is acceptable to individual or if it can be expanded.	Abstracted figure or landscape or non-objective fluid atmosphere using line and opaque washes. Emphasis on special continuity (viewing whole first) over focalized figure-ground relationship (dominant figure or design against field).
16. Oil-like handling.	Duplicate visual effect of ALLA PRIMA oil with polymer even though polymer has different "feel."	Realist approach using medium-heavy paint from tube. Emphasize brush handling, blending of color, mixing of polymer on palette. Work has to be fast and sure.
17. Oil-like handling.	Same as above.	Abstract approach relying on paint character and color to produce spatial differences: back-, middle-, and fore-ground. Express personal relation to paint surface. Reactive.
18. Glazing.	Produce oil-like glazing techniques. Explore brilliancy and intensity of polymer glazes.	Either realist or non-objective. Use transparent glazes over pure white surface, over other glazes, over opaque color ground, over slight textural painting. Dark or translucent glazes. Combine all for continuity through glazed optical values and contrast of subdued and intense color (or hot vs. cold).
19. Oil-like impasto.	Achieve heavy application of paint permanently and directly.	Use painting knives and brushes to produce heavy textural surface with paint only. Cut, clean edges contrasted with textural mass. Make polarities work.
20. Paint impasto.	Use paint to discover textural nature and fast working possibilities of polymer.	Build linear structure with 3-D line (knife or squeeze bottle application), and contrast with flat areas and textural paint. Use glazes and washes over to emphasize if desired. Incised line into heavy paint can vary approach.

MEDIA	SUPPORT	REFERENCE
Jar color thinned with water. Soft brushes in limited use to push color around or throw color on.	Raw cotton, stretched or unstretched.	Chapter 5, Staining and Fluid Color Fig. 28. Color Page 64.
Jar color. Variety of brushes.	Raw cotton duck.	Chapter 5 Figs. 28, 29, 30.
Tube color with only slight bit of water to thin. Oil bristle brushes or nylon.	Primed canvas.	Chapter 6 Figs. 31, 32, 36, 63. Color Page 82.
Same as above.	Primed canvas.	Chapter 6 Figs. 1, 35, 36, 64.
Tube or jar color combined with great amount of gloss medium.	Primed canvas, Masonite or Upsom board.	Chapter 6 Figs. 32, 37, 42, 55, 58, 59, 60, 65.
Tube color, painting knives, bristle and nylon brushes.	Sanded Masonite, stretched canvas, stretched burlap.	Chapter 6 Figs. 1, 42, 43, 57.
Tube color, painting knives, squeeze bottles, various brushes, sticks, etc.	Sanded Masonite, or canvas, or cloth backed to hardboard, using gel.	Chapters 6 and 7 Figs. 1, 42, 43.

TECHNIQUE APPROACH	PROBLEM	SUGGESTED DIRECTION
21. Textural additives with polymer paints and mediums.	Explore use of textural additives as direct paint or as textural grounds for painting.	a. Use non-objective or abstracted subject (try **NOT** to get textural materials to duplicate nature: the "feel" of the subject, yes; detailed duplication, no). Try as many additives as approach suggests with mediums and paint. Linear, fibrous or granular in combination. b. Prepare a textural ground for washes and stains and glazes of color. Contrast with flat areas if desired. Keep color muted. Use graffito or graffiti in wet build-ups if desired.
22. Mixed Media used with polymer.	Explore other materials which can be used for specific problems with with polymer.	a. Use re-soluble tempera with polymer and mediums to create a reworkable surface. Try for depth of color—dark scrubbed out to light. Literal give and take from painting surface. b. Use graphic materials, raw pigment to create polymer paint by addition of gloss medium.
23. Collage.	Use polymer mediums and collage elements primarily, with paint secondary.	Illusionism and spatial problems to be solved with collage experimentation. Direction can be two-dimensional or three-dimensional using flat or textural elements or combinations of both. Also use of repeated motif. Spatial continuity emphasis.
24. Sculptural using additives, collage, and including the two-dimensional painting surface.	Explore polymer and additive material in judgment of what is painting vs. what is sculpture and how to combine them, or if they can be combined effectively.	a. Using mediums, additives, and color. Project forms from two-dimensional surface and relate to the surface. b. Use multi-canvas approach, either one behind the other or, say, four canvases that can be combined by hanging together or by free standing in any 3D pattern. c. Free-standing sculpture developed from painterly viewpoint.
25. Printing and plate build-up (optional).	Use of collage and painting to develop a print surface.	a. Student choice as directed by previous explorations with polymer. b. Monoprints with polymer or stencil printing or silk-screening.
26. Mixed media and/or polymer extensions.	Diverse techniques dictated by previous explorations and search to find new innovations.	None. Student should be compelled to do a series of four or more innovational works in personal, imaginative, problem-solving experience. Use of new techniques not necessary, but valuable. Extension of techniques as personal development mandatory.

MEDIA	SUPPORT	REFERENCE
Tube color or jar color, gel medium, gloss medium, matte medium, gesso. Knives, brushes, sticks, etc. Sand, Celite, pumice, paper, cloth, powdered fiberglass, wood chips, sawdust, string, yarn, etc.	Sanded Masonite, Upsom board, fabric over hardboard using gel.	Chapters 6, 7, and 8 Figs. 3, 44, 45, 65.
Tube and/or jar colors, mediums. Tempera paint, raw pigment, pastels, charcoal, inks, etc.	Stretched canvas or open fabric such as burlap. Lots of "tooth" for graphic media.	Chapters 6, 7, and 8 Figs. 4, 36, 37, 38, 55, 56, 57, 59, 60.
Polymer mediums, gesso. Tube or jar color. Paper and cloth of every kind.	Masonite or rigid support.	Chapters 6 and 8 Figs. 46, 47, 48, 49, 50, 54, 56.
Jar and/or tube color. Mediums, additive materials including collage. Mixed media. All student choice directed by concept.	Several canvases which relate in form or in the concept of form.	Chapter 6 Figs. 51, 52, 53, 54. Color Page 82.
Modeling paste, mediums. Textural additives and collage elements. A good press is necessary with collagraphy.	Masonite panel or heavy matte board coated with gloss medium front and back.	Chapter 9 Figs. 66 through 75. Color Page 99.
Student choice.	Student choice.	Student choice or none.

5

Polymer Emulsions: The Water-dispersed Paint

The fact that polymer emulsions are basically water paints is often completely overlooked by artists. They consider them as another type of oil paint, or a material completely unrelated to water-suspended media. In doing so the artist ignores one of the inherent characteristics of the materials. Many of the traditional as well as the newer directions in art today are based on the direct acceptance of polymer emulsions as water-manipulated media that dry to a permanent surface. The effects of watercolor, tempera, and casein can be achieved, and all the techniques or traditional gimmicks associated with these materials can be used. But the resulting surface is permanent and water-insoluble. This fact, of course, leads to newer directions and further extensions of media esthetics.

This chapter will be concerned with direct, water-dispersion techniques, from traditional to contemporary. It is suggested that the artist use polymer emulsion jar colors for all techniques covered in this chapter. Although the thicker tubed colors can be employed, they are not as easily thinned and do not give the maximum brilliancy, opacity, or permanency because greater quantities of water must be used with the tubed colors to achieve fluid consistency.

Watercolor Effects

The Traditional Approach. When polymer emulsion colors are thinned greatly with water they handle in much the same way as watercolors. Dry brush, wash, and wet-in-wet techniques are created in the watercolor manner. The same drying times apply. The same brushes and papers are employed to the same ends. These approaches can be seen in Figures 6 and 7. If the reader needs a complete guide to watercolor techniques in the traditional sense, a book on watercolor should be consulted.

The Exceptions to the Rule. Polymer emulsion watercolors present several exceptions to the usual watercolor rules, however. First, the intensity of color and color values change when the thinned, wet color dries. This is also true with traditional watercolor, but the changes are not the same: polymer watercolors dry to a much higher degree of pigment intensity than traditional watercolors. Therefore the artist, when first approaching the polymer wash, will have to experiment to observe the exact color changes and readjust his preconceived color values to accommodate the new medium. As with watercolor, this becomes second nature in a short time. A rule of thumb is to add about twice as much water to the polymer jar color as you would to a tubed watercolor to achieve the same color value in drying.

Second, polymer colors dry water-insoluble and permanent. Colors can not be re-wet or reworked.

This prevents overworking and muddying of colors and leads to unusual techniques that cannot be achieved with traditional watercolor. Washes of transparent color can be made one over the other or over painted grounds without picking up the dry, underlying work. A new and unique sense of depth with multi-level applications lends a new dimension to watercolor paintings.

Also due to the permanency of the polymer watercolor surface, watercolors can be corrected by giving two or three opaque washes of Titanium White or polymer gesso, which will completely cover the work underneath and present a new surface on which to work. This technique can also be employed to tone down certain areas or provide atmospheric conditions, such as fog.

Wrinkled watercolor paper is never a problem when using polymer emulsion colors. Taping paper to heavy boards is not necessary. Polymers do not buckle papers as much as traditional watercolor because less water and more medium is usually employed. However, if in wet-in-wet techniques the paper buckles, let it; if the paper remains wrinkled when it dries, wet the back of the dry watercolor (and the front if necessary) until it is thoroughly saturated. Water will not affect the dry paint surface. Then place the watercolor under a clean piece of wood or heavy Masonite, larger than the painting. When the paper dries it will dry flat. Because little air can get to the paper under the board, it may take two days for drying.

There is an exception to the exception here, however: if a polymer watercolor is done *very* wet-in-wet, with large quantities of water and little color, the polymer binder may be washed out of

Figure 6. PENNY, 30 x 32 inches, by Russell Woody. Medium: LIQUITEX. Here synthetic emulsion was handled as a traditional-type watercolor wash. Lines were first drawn in with water-thinned Mars Black and a homemade reed pen. Washes of color over the dry, roughly-textured watercolor paper completed the work. (I mixed a tube of Cadmium Yellow watercolor paint with the LIQUITEX colors, because I was out of the emulsion Cadmium. The aqueous synthetics may be combined with most other water-based colors, including temperas and caseins; they impart the synthetics' characteristics of permanency and adhesion to the media to which they are added.) A coat of LIQUITEX MATTE VARNISH was then applied to protect the unpainted paper and retain the matte quality of a watercolor. I have used this work as a technical example in many lectures. Because of constant handling, it needed washing with soap and water several times, yet no damage is evident.

Figure 7. OUTPOST. 18 x 24 inches, by Barclay Sheaks. Medium: **NEW MASTERS** Illustrators' Colors. Inexpensive supports can be used in polymer work as the medium tends to protect the surface. Here a cheap, gray, sulphite construction paper was used. It was soaked completely in water, then spread flat on a piece of tempered Masonite so it would remain flat in the working process. No taping is necessary because the water adheres the paper to the board. Washes were then flowed into the wet surface; most of them quite opaque in order to achieve very rich bleeds and blendings of color. Work continued until the paper was dry.

When the watercolor was completely dry a mixture of 50% gloss medium and 50% water was brushed over the paint surface and on the back of the painting. The paper was so porous that the medium mixed with water seemed to penetrate through the paper. A coating of this sort was done to preserve the paper, otherwise the cheap paper would become brittle in a few years. Sheaks states that all his tests indicate this to be a safe method.

The "varnish-coating" over the watercolor leaves a slight sheen, but no gloss. Similar effects can be achieved on rice paper but Sheaks prefers the cheap gray paper because it absorbs great quantities of water. The paper yellows on aging and both the translucence and the opaque colors tend to brighten instead of darken, producing a lovely mellowing effect, which Sheaks wants. More transparent colors would tend to change color as the paper yellowed.

the paint and then the surface will no longer be water insoluble. It would be a good rule to add a slight amount of polymer gloss medium to the paints when working in this manner. After the fluid painting is dry, spray or lightly brush on a coat of matte varnish to insure durability.

Transparent Colors. There are inherently opaque as well as inherently transparent pigments in all media. If very transparent washes are desired the following colors give the best results in watercolor techniques: Yellow Light Hansa, Yellow Medium Azo, Yellow Orange Azo, Indo Orange Red, Napthol ITR Red Light, Napthol ITR Crimson, Phthalocyanine Green, Hookers Green, Phthalocyanine Blue, Ultramarine Blue, and Linear Quinacridone Red and Violet. Other colors such as Cadmiums can be used with greater amounts of water added.

Some of the more opaque colors show pigment separation when diluted too freely with water. This is caused by loss of medium (in traditional as well as polymer watercolors). If this occurs on the palette or the paper, a few drops of matte varnish or gloss medium will correct the fault. A proper binder-pigment ratio has to be maintained.

Resist and Unusual Techniques. Since polymer emulsions are water paints, they can be used with the usual materials to repel water to achieve a white space, a clearly defined line, or splotching. Rubber cement, turpentine, wax, crayons, clear oils, and oil pastels are only a few of the media used in resist. Figure 8 illustrates a wash resist drawing.

Of course the artist should not limit himself to any set pattern, mechanical method, or any "correct" prescription of tools, materials, or supports. Anything that serves the artist's purpose is "correct." Areas can be masked out with tapes and stencils. White lines can be scratched with knives and razor blades. Graphic media (pencils, ink, charcoal, etc.) can be used and fixed with a spray of half medium and half water to keep them from bleeding or smearing—or allowed to bleed or blend.

Figure 9, by artist and teacher *Barclay Sheaks,* shows what can be accomplished with a graphic wash. Although the line here is water soluble, a definitive and permanent line can be produced with certain types of indelible felt marking pens. This type of line is not only water insoluble but it will always bleed through polymer. Twenty coats of paint can go over the line and the line will bleed through to the top so the graphic design is never lost. Occasionally painters make the mistake of using these pens to mark the title of the painting on the back of absorbent papers and canvas. Much to their surprise and chagrin, the title is on the surface of the painting, in reverse, the next day.

Mediums Used with Polymer Watercolor. The artist can control a polymer watercolor with much more precision by the use of polymer mediums than in the traditional approach. The addition of medium in various quantities controls the flow of the paint, allowing some areas to bleed freely while others are restricted; the more medium used (either gloss or matte varnish), the less the color will flow.

The process is generally wet-in-wet, with heavy watercolor paper being *saturated* with a half-and-half mixture of water and gloss medium. Matte medium or matte varnish can be used for less surface sheen. After the medium-water mixture has thoroughly soaked into the paper, washes of color thinned with water can be applied. These feather and spread in the normal watercolor manner. Semi-opaque color can be used over the fluid washes and controlled by blotting and tilting the work and by adding more medium to stop the spread of color at certain points. Final opaque accents are painted in while the paper is still moist. A final semi-matte varnish, of matte varnish and gloss medium mixed, can be brushed on over the dry permanent watercolor surface to give an over-all sheen.

Figure 8. WOMAN A 41, 18 x 24 inches, by Russell Woody. Media: LIQUITEX and oil. This drawing, done with LIQUITEX, purposely violates one of the few rules of painting with the synthetic emulsions. It has been said throughout this book that oil should never be mixed with the aqueous emulsions. In this case, several drops of linseed oil were mixed with LIQUITEX Mars Black, slightly thinned with water and medium to form a thick ink. A bamboo pen was used. The spotty textures in the tonal washes were caused by the oil resisting the LIQUITEX. The unmixability of oil with synthetic paints creates a mess to clean in the brush, but the possible effects are very unusual.

Figure 9. UNTITLED line and acrylic wash, 12 x 18 inches, by Barclay Sheaks. Medium: LIQUITEX. Using gray construction paper, the subject was sketched in with a lithograph pencil. (Lithograph crayons and pencils are water soluble—a thin wash is repelled by the line but fluid washes will dissolve it so the litho line can be blended into the painting or completely removed by scrubbing with water.) Painting continued with thin opaque as well as transparent washes of polymer color applied over the litho drawing. In some areas the paints were laid on thickly to give a heavier paint texture in combination with the line. Since the crayon draws beautifully over dried and nearly dried acrylic, the work was finished in this manner.

A varnish of full strength gloss medium was applied to preserve the paper and to set the water-soluble line into the polymer surface. To do this, Sheaks rolled the medium over the work with a rubber brayer. This takes skill and a quick hand. Two sprays of medium and water might work more easily for those not accustomed to this technique. The brayer leaves a semi-gloss and a slightly pebbled finish, which Sheaks prefers. Some method of quick application has to be used, however, because the litho crayon will dissolve and muddy the painting if a brush is used with heavy medium.

Sheaks frames this type of work under glass because the crayon, even with a varnish of medium, can be easily scratched and is almost impossible to repair.

Opaque Watercolor; Gouache. When Titanium White is added to polymer jar colors in small amounts the result is opaque watercolor, or, traditionally, gouache. If thinned with water, the more opaque polymer colors work well for this technique. In the past, gouache could not be piled up heavily without risk of cracking. Now the plastic paints permit any amount of dense paint films without cracking, even on light-weight paper.

Tempera and Casein

The body of polymer emulsion colors as they come from the jar is between the viscosity of tempera and casein, depending upon the brand. If too thick for tempera manipulations, thin with water; if too thin for casein work an inert additive may be mixed in; or switch to tubed polymer and thin with water. Inert clays to be used include Celite, diatomaceous earth, or any type of powdered silica and whiting (Calcium Carbonate—Paris White). These materials are first mixed with gloss medium to the consistency of the paint desired and then added to the color. If medium is not used the resulting paint will be brittle.

The quality of traditional egg tempera is achieved by mixing the yolk of an egg in the proportions of one or two parts yolk to three parts jar color. Warm water facilitates the blend-

Figure 10. Polymer emulsion on paper (demonstration). Polymer emulsion colors were used directly from the jar to simulate casein. The paint was applied in five minutes, using dry brush as well as fluid technique.

Figure 11. Polymer emulsion on-paper correction (demonstration). After ten minutes drying time areas can be painted out completely with Titanium White for corrections. Or the whole painting can be done over. Thirty paintings a day can be completed, one over the other. In this approach to painting, good technique is easily acquired.

ing. Brushes are dipped into water and then into the egg and color mixture. This type of egg tempera is permanent and can be applied to flexible surfaces such as canvas. Thomas Hart Benton uses the egg-base synthetic tempera technique for his easel paintings. The transparency and the resulting depth that the medium achieves suit his work very well.

Water-thinned polymers dry matte and therefore change to a lower color intensity, as do tempera and casein. If the original "wet" color value is desired then a coat of gloss medium is given to the dried painting and the approximate degree of "wet" refraction and reflection is restored. The artist has to make the decision as to a glossy, very intense color value or a relative matte surface duplicating the tempera-casein effect.

The basic difference between traditional tempera-casein painting and the polymer approach is the one of permanency. Any support mentioned in the section on basic supports for polymers can be used. This means the artist can paint in a casein or tempera manner on canvas and, due to the somewhat spurious buying habits of the public, sell the work for more money. Paint on canvas, regardless of quality of work, many times means more money.

Drying time for polymer tempera-casein applications depends upon the thickness of the paint. Normal films will dry water-insoluble in about twenty minutes. It follows that the artist needs good technique; the medium demands it. But the best part of painting in this manner—especially for the beginner—is that overpainting can be accomplished almost immediately. Corrections are possible every twenty minutes or so. This is illustrated in Figures 10 and 11.

The magic realism of *Louis Jones* has the surface appearance of tempera, casein, and, at times, oil. Much like all outstanding artists working in this esthetic approach, the realism comes last; the basic painting is abstract.

Typical of his working techniques is THE MEATS AND THE POISONS, Color Page 49. Jones usually uses quarter-inch sanded Masonite panels or paper board as a support. This one was done on bristol board taped down to reduce warp and covered with approximately five coats of polymer gesso. The gesso was thinned with water (one part water to three parts gesso) and sanded between each coat, the last application left unsanded to increase absorbency and pull. A drawing of the subject was executed in pencil and isolated with a coat of gloss medium to prevent pickup. Often Jones does not use preliminary drawings but lets the work develop as forms are created with loose abstract color work.

At this point intense washes and glazes of color were thrown onto the support to establish basic light and dark relationships. These were isolated with medium, and the basic, but very brilliant and intense, colors were brushed on to establish modeling. The intensity of these first colors was reduced by many over-glazes, which finished the painting process. By using such brilliant color in the preliminary work, a greater, but subtle, richness of color results throughout.

The glazes—four to ten layers are usual—were applied spontaneously with rags, newspapers, and almost anything but a brush. Jones states that this tends to avoid the usual overworked feeling that a magic realist approach too often fosters. Occasionally he uses a brush to pick out highlights and for retouching and bringing out detail in the latter phases of the work, but he tries to avoid the brush as much as possible in color development. Color was scrubbed away in the drying process with rags, etc., in each coat. The more color the artist wanted to remain, the longer the glaze was allowed to dry before it was rubbed or picked off.

Each glaze was isolated with gloss medium before other work proceeded. This achieves a greater depth and brilliance of color even in the earth colors that Jones relies on quite heavily.

Much of Louis Jones' work is done on "location," such as WINDOW LIGHT, Figure 12, done in the bathroom at Cranbrook Institute. Jones writes: "I have a small set of polymer emulsion squeeze tubes, which I keep in a wooden box named 'Herman,' and he goes with me on every trip. They are great for on spot work. I used 'Herman' in the bathroom at Cranbrook (where the window was) without the usual mess oils would have made."

Jones continues, "I feel that polymers are the medium of an art future which promises to blur into non existence the often times rather artificial division between painting, sculpture, assemblage."

Since Jones is also a college professor his views should be noted. He says that "the medium gives the student a potential of achieving a range of expression with one medium only attainable in the past with the mastery of a dozen or more materials. It gives almost complete technical freedom and it does not involve a lot of useless folderol and hocus pocus to achieve some rather elementary aesthetic statements. Also the low cost factor, durability, ease of use and speed in handling are all advantageous to the average college student. The only disadvantage is that the color range is not as varied as some would like as yet. However, I think most of the disadvantages people attribute to polymers are psychological in nature."

Figure 12. WINDOW LIGHT, approx. 36 x 54 inches, by Louis Jones. Medium: LIQUITEX. (Collection: George S. Frierson, Jr.) The painting was executed on quarter-inch untempered sanded Masonite and follows Jones' polymer tempera approach. About six coats of thinned polymer gesso formed the ground. Over this, very intense yellows and oranges were, literally, thrown. These fluid colors were allowed to dry while the painting was flat and then isolated with gloss medium. A coat of grey-green and blue was thrown on next and isolated. During each of the color applications the color was carefully dabbed away from the sunlit wall area to retain maximum reflection from the gesso ground. The final color consisted of a very light warm grey, overwashed with a hint of yellow oxide for more warmth when the painting proved to have too cold a cast. Work in this period was done with brush for detail and texture as well as direct throwing of color. No medium was mixed with the colors, only water, the first coat being quite fluid and the final coat rather thick in viscosity.

The painting has a nice glow unapparent in the black-and-white photograph as well as a subtle actual texture due to the brushwork. Areas of contrasting opacity and transparency give depth. The panel is braced on the back with 1- x 2-inch wood strips.

Figure 13. THE NEW ADAM, 24 x 48 inches, by
Louis Jones. Medium: LIQUITEX, (Courtesy: the
artist.) In this painting a gesso ground was used
for absorbency rather than whiteness. One thin coat
of polymer gesso was spottily applied over a pre-
vious ground of a Pthalocyanine Blue, Cadmium
Yellow Light, and Raw Umber mixture, which had
been opaquely painted over Jones' usual gessoed
Masonite support. This created a variegated color
ground with slightly differing absorptive powers. In
final glazes it allowed the artist to pick up more
paint in some areas than others when wet color was
wiped from the work with absorbent materials.

Texture in the rocks was created by picking up
color with crumpled rags and newspapers. Portions
of the rocks were accented with a brush and thin
paint mixed with gloss medium. The salt and pepper
shakers were rendered over the rock ground in
opaque polymer colors straight from the jar.

A final varnish of polymer matte varnish was
brushed on to bring the shakers into surface key
with the rest of the painting, since gloss medium
mixed with color gives a slight surface sheen similar
to matte varnish.

Figure 13, THE NEW ADAM, shows more
clearly the texture achieved by Jones' use of
crumpled newspapers and rags to pick up color
washes and glazes. Jones has exhibited widely
throughout the United States, is a member of the
National Association of Casein Painters, and
teaches art on the college level. His work is handled by The Arwin Galleries, Detroit, Michigan
and the Mint Museum of Art, Charlotte, N. C.

In opposition to Jones' work, artist *Barclay
Sheaks* approaches his tempera-like work with a
brush-stroke by brush-stroke application of color,
using fine-line brushes. There is no real secret
behind his technique: you just have to be good.
Figure 14 shows the result of fine craftsmanship.

The work of *Fairfield Porter* is more direct.
Structure and pattern are predominant as opposed
to modeling of figures and objects. STEPHEN
AND KATHY, Figure 15, shows his approach.
The canvas is primed with polymer gesso or medium, and thin transparent washes follow, which,
at times, contrast with opaque, heavier areas.
Sometimes Porter mixes matte medium in with
polymer colors along with water to thin them
without creating a textural surface but yet having
a heavier flow. He does not use a final varnish of
gloss medium as he prefers the soft matte surface
of the paint.

THE MEAT AND THE POISONS, 22 x 28 inches, by Louis Jones. Medium: LIQUITEX. (Courtesy: the artist.) This painting is typical of the artist's work, his subtle color relationships and balance between abstract and realism, lights and darks, transparency and opacity. The technique is described in the text.

Detail of THE AGES OF MEDICINE, mural by Tom Vincent. Medium: LIQUITEX and tempera paint. Vincent's painterly approach can be seen here, as well as the subtle texture created with gesso, medium, and modeling paste, Installation view of this large work (78 x 247 inches) and a full description are on pages 92-93.

Figure 14. RURAL TOTEM NO. 2, 36 x 48 inches, by Barclay Sheaks. Medium: NEW MASTERS Illustrators Color. (Courtesy: the artist.) The support for this painting is tempered Masonite sanded completely on the smooth side with medium-grain sandpaper to achieve a tooth to hold the acrylic ground. Two coats of acrylic gesso were applied with a brush and sanded slightly. The result was a smooth painting surface much like a traditional panel for traditional egg tempera painting.

Painting was direct-color applied with relatively small brushes. It was given two coats of gloss medium. Sheaks applies medium and varnishes with a rubber sgueegee to obtain a trackless, brushless and brilliant, smooth finish.

Figure 15. STEPHEN AND KATHY, 60 x 48 inches, by Fairfield Porter. Medium: LIQUITEX. (Courtesy: the artist; photograph by Ellen Auerbach.) Porter likes the effects of aqueous media such as casein, tempera, and watercolor, and this affinity is reflected in his polymer paintings. It enables him to work on canvas in a casein manner without the traditional medium's disadvantage of cracking. Furthermore, the synthetic pigments have created new color interplay and contrasts, especially in the pastel tints.

Beyond the Traditional

The extension of a permanent, water-suspended medium beyond the usual limitations of the traditional water media is quite obvious today in the areas labelled "Hard Edge," "Optical," or "Color Field" painting. But before polymer, the intensity of a flat color area was hard to achieve, and usually impossible to obtain if comparative permanency had to be maintained. The staining of raw canvas with a relatively permanent paint was almost out of the question. In fact, I doubt that some of these important directions would have developed to the point of prominence they enjoy today without the indirect "massage" of polymers.

The late Morris Lewis' work changed radically when he started using polymer. It would be highly debatable and unrealistic to pursue this statement and point of view to a conclusion that polymers direct the artist, but I am sure an influence is felt. Richard Anuszkiewicz has said that in changing his image approach to painting the polymer emulsions had a direct effect on his work even to the point of influencing the image. Allan D'Arcangelo's approach was, he states, "a very happy marriage in terms of what I wanted to do and the material (polymer emulsion) which did it best." Although Helen Lundeberg had developed a method of Hard Edge painting with oils, she switched to polymers because of their fast drying and more permanent surface. In her words: "A late (1965), but enthusiastic, convert."

The above comments are typical of many artists working with polymer emulsions—from those working in the non-objective field to those working traditionally. It is an understanding and acceptance of the basic properties of a medium and a rapport that develops between artist and materials that leads to areas beyond the material to the esthetic.

The Power of Color—Optical Approach.

Whatever the label—Post-Painterly Abstraction, Optical, or Hard Edge—the emphasis of the direction is on the medium. In painting, the optical quality and two-dimensionality is stressed as opposed to the tactile quality of sculpture. The expressive power of pure color dominates any painterly overtones.

Polymer colors, as extensions of the flat tempera technique, are uniquely suited to these approaches because of the innate optical brilliance they afford. They are not without technical problems however.

The works illustrated here are by outstanding professional artists who know their craft. They are "pros" in every sense of the word, know what they want, and spend endless hours in technical as well as creative search.

As an example, most of the artists working with intense flat color application and retaining hard-edge divisions of color apply thinned polymer emulsion colors with a brush. It is very hard for the student to get the same results. When using brush applications he will usually obtain streaks, bubbles, and varying intensities of color. To achieve a professional finish means hours of experimentation and hard work. Each artist has to work out his own answers. The following illustrations and suggestions should help.

Sprays. I would advise that the easiest way for the uninitiated to apply color is to use an air gun or air brush. The better the gun, the better the end result. A few suggestions as to type are made under *Varnishing,* in Chapter 3. Jar color is thinned with water (and/or medium) until a fine mist spray can be achieved. It will take up to five coats of color in this method of working to produce opacity. Care should be taken that the spray does not deposit "beads" of color on the support and that the unit does not "spit." An adjustable nozzle will usually eliminate these problems.

Tapes. Hard edges are most often obtained with tape and taped on paper masks. The type of tape used is critical. If the gummed side of the tape is too sticky the undercoats of paint will adhere more to the tape than to the support and color will be pulled from the support when the tape is stripped up. If the top surface of the tape is absorbent, the

CELESTIAL, 60 x 60 inches, by Richard Anuszkiewicz. Medium: LIQUITEX. (Courtesy: Sidney Janis Gallery, New York.) An example of the artist's approach with polymer emulsions as described in the text, pages 53-55.

paint may adhere more to the tape than the support and then areas along the tape edge will be pulled away, leaving anything but a hard edge—it will be more serrated than anything else.

The problem is that there is no one brand of tape that will do all jobs correctly, and brands and quality of tapes vary from area to area. A plastic tape used by commercial artists works well and is sold in plastic containers so circles and curves can be cut with ease. Some artists prefer a cloth tape with a non-textured surface because plastic tapes stretch at times causing unwanted curves. Cheap, crepe-paper type tapes should, for the most part, be avoided; they are usually too adhesive or tear easily. I have used electrical tape (3M Brand), which works well for my purposes. But, again, the rule is to experiment to find the type that will give the best result for the particular job the artist has at hand. Tapes will be discussed below from the artists' personal points of view.

Stripping of Tape. Because polymer colors are thinned greatly with water for most hard-edge applications, they lose some of their strength. This will cause the dry paint to strip up with the tape in some cases. To prevent this, and to stop seepage of paint under the tape, a coat of polymer gloss medium is brushed over the tape after it is applied and the medium is extended about two inches beyond the tape on either side. The whole surface of the painting can be isolated with medium after taping as well. Color is then applied.

For best results the tape should be pulled just after the color dries. The time is critical, and varies according to the thickness of color. Usually the waiting time is ten to fifteen minutes. With a few tries the artist will be able to judge time in relation to his particular application of color. If the tape is not removed at this time it is best to wait until the paint is completely dry—overnight or several hours—and then pull the line or edge.

The Artist's Approach. Richard Anuszkiewicz is one of the leaders in his field in the world of art today. His approach is personal as he feels every artist's should be.

"The technique should serve the image," he states. "Each artist should find the proper technique for his particular image and this is only done through experimentation. The technique, of course, does not make the painting but the technique must become the servant of the image and work with it. What is particularly exciting today is that there is no one technique or approach to painting."

His techniques may be helpful as a starting point for others.

Anuszkiewicz uses raw cotton duck as a support for almost all his work at this point. At one time he used braced Masonite panels for sizes less than four by four feet. Problems with tape pulling paint from an improper hardboard surface directed his switch to all canvas. He prefers cotton canvas over linen because it has a more even finish.

Three coats of polymer gesso are given to the canvas, with each coat sanded. Whatever color is decided for the "line" of the painting is then brushed on with large red sable and soft sabeline brushes. Approximately five coats of water-thinned polymer color are usually applied to achieve the intensity and opacity of color that Anuszkiewicz prefers. He finds very little trouble with bubbles forming, texture, or streaks when the paint is diluted to the proper flow consistency. A few colors tend to streak, he says, such as Phthalocyanine Green mixed with Titanium White, but with care this can be controlled.

When the color meets his standards it is allowed to dry thoroughly and varnished with thinned gloss medium. Anuszkiewicz varnishes every color layer to prevent any bleed or muddying of color in succeeding color applications. Since the paint is greatly diluted with water some pick-up of color may result from loss of medium if a varnish is not applied. The artist uses a sponge for varnishing, to cover the large areas quickly and to avoid brush strokes.

Tapes are rubbed onto the varnished color field as in Figures 16 and 17. In intricate patterns,

Figure 16. Painting in progress, no. 1, by Richard Anuszkiewicz. Medium: LIQUITEX. (Courtesy: the artist.) The gloss areas faintly seen extending from the tapes indicate the application of gloss medium over the tape and adjacent areas to prevent bleeding and seepage of color under the tape. Anuszkiewicz's paintings are worked horizontally and suspended on saw horses. The painting shown here can be seen in its work position in the background of Figure 18.

Figure 18. Palette arrangement, Richard Anuszkiewicz. (Courtesy: the artist.) It may look haphazard and unusual, but the colors for paintings are all premixed in containers carefully marked and keyed to paintings in progress or finished. The traditional approach to palette mixtures would be impossible in Anuszkiewicz's work.

Figure 17. Painting in progress, no. 2. Anuszkiewicz demonstrates his measuring device to assure correct spacing between charting tapes. Although the tapes are sometimes readjusted by eye, perfection is the objective in his modular squares.

the artist prepares a modular measuring device to make sure the units of design are precise. Figure 17 shows Anuszkiewicz checking grid systems in this manner. The dark line is tape, not paint. It will be removed after another application of color. The artist prefers charting tapes to the masking tapes he previously used. They work better and are available in very fine widths. In the change-over, Anuszkiewicz says, this allowed for complex grids and linear systems that altered his approach to the modular image.

Palette arrangement and color mixing are very different from the traditional. Colors are all pre-mixed in containers before painting begins. (See Figure 18.)

Because of the color change that polymer paints exhibit on drying and because varnish also changes the color intensity, the artist *must* know exactly what is going to happen to the color in its final state. This requires a second nature knowledge of all drying characteristics of all colors; otherwise the artist must pre-test all color mixtures.

Anuszkiewicz does not make a fetish out of this process but he does quickly test colors and their color relationships (an integral part of his work) by painting out colors side by side and over one another and then varnishing them. His method can be seen in Figure 19. The color swatch above the painting is the key for color application in the work below. Colors can be adjusted in the painting process, of course, but a standard for working relationships needs to be established first.

Overpainting can easily and quickly change the direction of the work, and Anuskiewicz does much overpainting. But all his work is based on a sound working knowledge of exact color relationships.

When complete, his paintings are given a final varnish of gloss medium or matte varnish applied with a sponge.

CELESTIAL, Color Page 52, illustrates the final product of Anuskiewicz's approach.

A combination of Expressionism and Hard Edge is seen in the work of *Nicholas Krushenick*. His paintings have also been listed in anthologies

Figure 19. Color tests for painting, by Richard Anuszkiewicz. Medium: LIQUITEX. (Courtesy: the artist.) Color tests to determine color value and intensity of polymers when they dry or when they are varnished are mandatory in close optical relationships. This painting by Anuszkiewicz is controlled by the paint-outs tacked to the wall of the studio above the work.

Coverage is checked under a good light. Some colors require a white underneath to produce maximum color effects.

on Pop Art, although he does not personally identify with this. Krushenick started using polymers in 1960 and has stated that he could not now go back to oils. Without polymer emulsions, he says, he could not get the sustained brilliancy and matte quality he desires.

Krushenick paints on a gesso ground applied directly to raw canvas. Sometimes a coat of matte medium or Titanium White is painted over (or used instead of) the gesso in order to reduce the pull and semi-absorbent properties of gesso. Emulsion colors with a little water are painted very flatly over the ground. Many of his paintings, such as Figure 20, PAINTING, 1963, have many coats and shifts of areas before the painting is complete.

STEEPLECHASE, Color Page 61, is unusual in that the shaped support is a mahogany-finished veneer mounted over a frame ribbing of pine—somewhat similar in construction to a hollow door. It was cut with a small, electric saber-saw and constructed in two basic sections, bolted together at the center. Fine cracks were filled with polymer modeling paste sanded to create a smooth surface.

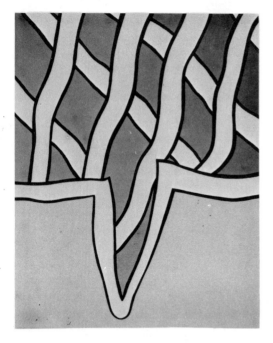

Figure 20. PAINTING 1963, 45 x 52 inches, by Nicholas Krushenik. Medium: LIQUITEX. (Courtesy: the artist.) Executed on raw linen canvas primed with polymer gesso. Six to eight coats of paint were applied in the process of shifting and re-shifting the composition. A little water was added to the colors to achieve smooth brushing qualities. The blue, red, oranges, and blacks of the painting are very flat, very matte, very intense in color. No final varnish was given.

Two coats of sanded synthetic gesso were brushed on as a ground. Then polymer colors slightly thinned with water were brushed on. Lines were cut with masking tape. An isolating coat of gloss medium was applied between each color application to facilitate tape removal. No final varnish was given.

The painting was designed to be hung flush with the ceiling so the color will seem to come through and thrust down into the room below.

Some of the most saturated, intense, and lyrical color I have seen is illustrated in WATER-WAYS, Color Page 64, by the West Coast artist *Helen Lundeberg,* whose works have been exhibited in major museums in this country and at the Sao Paulo Biennial, and whose paintings are in many important collections, including the San Francisco Museum of Art, the Los Angeles Museum, and the Hirshhorn Collection. Miss Lundeberg's work is handled by the David Stuart Galleries in Los Angeles.

Miss Lundeberg moved from oil to polymers for the durability and fast working properties of polymer. To achieve her effects the polymer colors are thinned with water and brushed onto a Titanium White primed cotton duck. Brushes used are of the wide, thin, short natural bristle, sign-painter type. To avoid brush marks, thin spots, and bubbles the paint is worked generously onto the surface while turning the brush in several directions. Then the paint is smoothed by brushing all in one direction. If any unwanted effects do occur the area is simply repainted.

Vital to Lundeberg's approach is proper paint consistency, but, as she says, "How can you describe that?" It is a question well taken. The artist has to derive his own rapport with (and from) the materials for his own image.

Lundeberg tapes color areas with Scotch Brand Masking Tape #202 and usually applies two coats of paint to achieve proper color value. No isolating coats of medium are used. (See Figure 21, PLANET No. 5.)

The hard edge does not have to be cut with tape. *Carl Swallow,* another West Coast artist,

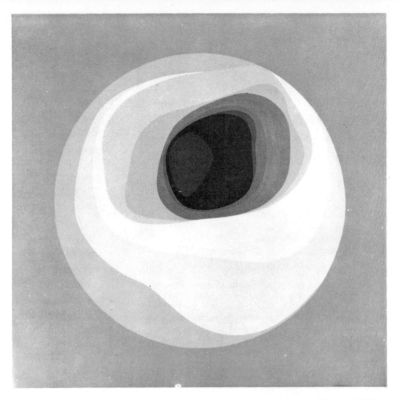

Figure 21. PLANET NO. 5, 60 x 60 inches, by Helen Lundeberg. Medium: LIQUITEX. (Courtesy: the artist.) Although technically similar in approach to WATER-WAYS, Color Page 64, a different visual impact is produced here. Lundeberg finds transparent polymer colors harder to control and she tends to use the "gay" colors sparingly, if at all. She advises that a spot of color should never be retouched until the paint film is thoroughly dry.

often uses a brush for sharp edges, as can be seen in Figure 22. ORIGINAL AMERICAN MANDALLA has a support of cotton duck and is primed with Sears Acrylic Latex (exterior). The acrylic polymer colors used *(Liquitex)* are compatible with this commercial house paint. They were thinned with matte medium and applied directly with small sign-painting brushes to achieve the effect illustrated.

The sometimes Pop imagery of *Allan D'Arcangelo* is controlled by this outstanding artist's almost "second nature" use of polymer emulsions. He was introduced to the materials in 1958, in Mexico City, where synthetics were first really explored by artists. He began using them to save money: a good permanent paint that could be used on paper. When D'Arcangelo returned to the United States and began explorations toward his present directions, polymer colors were the perfect answer to the very impersonal kind of surface and sharp edges he wanted, in direct contrast to the Abstract Expressionists. Thus he had a solid technical background with which to exploit the materials. An early work, LANDSCAPE 1964, is reproduced in Chapter 7, "Mixed Media and Polymer."

Figure 22. ORIGINAL AMERICAN MANDALLA, 48 x 48 inches, by Carl Swallow. Medium: LIQUITEX and SEARS ACRYLIC LATEX. (Courtesy: the artist.) The hard edge can be cut with brushes as well as tape, as shown here. Good quality sign-painters' brushes are useful to produce the precise edges (Stripers, Dagger Stripers, and Sable Fitches work well).

D'Arcangelo prefers nylon bristle brushes in a width only manufactured as house-paint brushes. (See Figure 23.) They give better pressure, he states, and the pressure used is quite important. He advises a very light touch to prevent streaking, using only one-quarter inch of the bristles in contact with the canvas.

The artist has used spray units for some work, especially sculptural pieces, but still prefers the brush because, he states, spray units clog too easily and their use requires more coats of paint.

The technique of D'Arcangelo is illustrated in Figure 24, one of his popular "Road" or "Landscape" paintings. The support is cotton duck covered with three coats of sanded gesso, the gesso applied in a very water-dilute consistency. Areas were masked out with tape and several coats of each color brushed on. Translucent colors and certain reds and yellows take up to six coats to give the surface and intensity the artist wants.

D'Arcangelo does not recommend any one brand of tape but does insist that experience with a particular type must be gained for proper results. Bleeding and seepage is controlled by rubbing the tape with a burnishing tool to assure proper contact with the ground. "Or the easiest thing to do," he says, "is to coat the tape with polymer medium and rub it under the tape with your thumb while it is still wet, take any excess off, and then press down the tape with your fingernail. Once in a while there is some seepage with this technique, but it can be touched up easily."

Work following the "Highway" and "Grass" series is illustrated in Figure 25 and LANDSCAPE 1968, Color Page 61. The technique is the same. His new work may take on a decidedly different shape. (See Figure 26.)

D'Arcangelo has used almost all types of supports, including wood, hardboard, Plexiglas, glass, cotton and linen canvas, and paper. He even painted the side of an old building on Ninth Street between First and Second Avenues in New York. After two years the polymer painting was still in excellent condition.

His main problem in any case seems to be lap marks. To prevent this he has to work fast—*very* fast on large canvases.

He states: "You have to work wet-in-wet at all times or lap marks result. In doing the large painting for Expo (21 feet long and 11 feet high) it took two of us to do it. Most of it is one solid color—light blue—and we took three hours to to get one coat on, working wet into wet, pulling it out. Consistency of paint is important. I try to get all colors to the consistency of milk, using only water to thin the color.

"When you tell a student to work fast," he continues, "the student has no conception of what you mean. The student thinks he is working fast and you look and know it's not fast enough. Work in large color areas has to be furious."

To produce his almost Pop portrait work, artist *Barkley Sheaks* uses an air brush. Sheaks states

Figure 23. Allan D'Arcangelo's studio wall, showing his selection and care of brushes. The plastic containers are cut to hold the nylon brushes in water without bending the bristles.

Figure 24. HIGHWAY 1, NO. 4, 70 x 81 inches, by Allan D'Arcangelo. Medium: LIQUITEX. (Courtesy: Fischback Gallery; Collection, John Powers.) D'Arcangelo's HIGHWAY series is typical of his direct water-thinned polymer approach.

that he employs the air brush to achieve more color power, or color and optical vibration. It is about the only way, he says, that he can obtain the mechanical, pure color areas he wants and have them uncorrupted by slight, but obvious, brush marks.

Sheaks' support for spray paintings is sanded, one-eighth-inch tempered Masonite with two coats of polymer gesso. All basic colors are painted on with bristle brushes. These are flat color areas without shading or modeling. The color is very much diluted with water, requiring up to five coats to produce the color power needed.

The basics are done with a brush to save the airbrush for its best purpose and to do away with unnecessary and lengthy spraying. Straight edges are masked with tape and free form shapes are cut from paper. Sheaks recommends tracing paper or butchers' paper as both are transparent enough to

Figure 25. Painting in progress, by Allan D'Arcangelo. Medium: LIQUITEX. (Courtesy: the artist.) This shows the artist's somewhat free development of color areas. Although the method may look haphazard, D'Arcangelo produces technically perfect paintings. The reader would do better to follow more exacting and careful manipulations until he has the experience of this artist—which is over ten years in polymer techniques.
　　Linear vanishing points for the beams, drawn on the gessoed canvas, can be faintly seen.

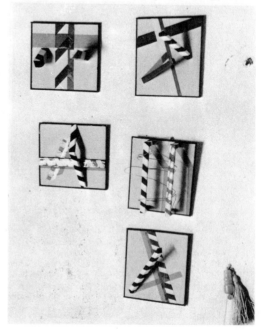

Figure 26. Studies for a future work hang on the wall of Allan D'Arcangelo's studio. The forms literally project from the surface of the painting. The support for this work will be braced plywood; the projecting forms will also be wood. The wood will be gessoed and painted with water-thinned polymer emulsion colors.

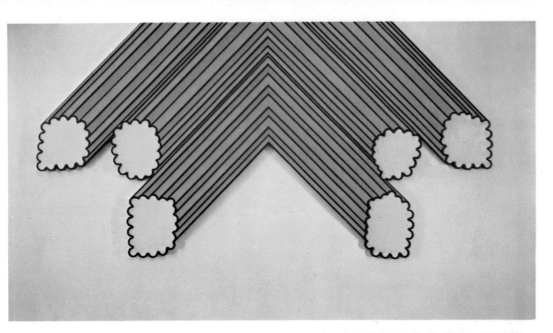

STEEPLECHASE, 97 x 189 inches, by Nicholas Krushenik. Medium: LIQUITEX on shaped mahogany veneer. (Courtesy: Pace Gallery; photograph by F. Boesch. Collection: Walker Art Center, Minneapolis.) Krushenik designed this painting to be hung flush with the ceiling so the color will seem to thrust down into the room below. Fully described in the text, under "Beyond the Traditional."

LANDSCAPE 1968, 54 x 48 inches, by Allan D'Arc-angelo. Medium: LIQUITEX. (Courtesy: the artist.) The final result of a start as shown in Figure 25. D'Arcangelo never uses a final varnish of any kind because he does not like the color and depth change it produces. Color is worked from light to dark. For example, in yellow and red, the whole shape is masked off and painted yellow—with as many as four or five coats. Then the red is masked and painted over the yellow. It is a matter of building up layers, always working from light to dark. The yellow underneath produces a nice resonance in the red. In one sense, it is almost a glazing technique, except that the many over coats of color render it almost opaque.

Figure 27. MY CAR, BARBARA, 36 x 48 inches, by Barclay Sheaks. Medium: NEW MASTERS Illustrators Colors. (Courtesy: the artist.) Sheaks uses a Binks air brush with the WREN A and WREN B model brushes for his spray paintings. The compresser is also a Binks, designed for use with the above models. Colors are greatly thinned with water and a bit of medium to a consistency that will go through the nozzle of the air brush. All colors are strained through silk or nylon mesh after they are mixed, and just before spraying, to achieve a uniform consistency and to prevent clogging of the spray unit.

A final varnish of about four coats of gloss medium thinned with water is sprayed on to complete the work.

place over an area and trace the outlines to be masked. The paper is then cut with a utility knife and fastened to areas with *3M Spray Adhesive* in the temporary bond technique described on the spray container. Areas are then modeled and shadowed with the air brush. (See Figure 27.)

Staining and Fluid Color. About the only way to produce intense, permanent stains of paint on canvas is to use synthetics. Polymer emulsion paints seem to sink into raw canvas and become one with it. Because of the nature of the material the artist can achieve an effect where the foreground and background seem to become one. The color "floats."

Successive sprays or stains of color cause the colors to "melt" into one another creating a fluid, brilliant, saturated atmosphere. Jules Olitski both sprays and stains. William Pettet sprays. Helen Frankenthaler stains.

Frankenthaler, using polymer emulsions for their special aqueous quality, first investigated them for their permanency on raw, unsized canvas. The unique results of her investigations can be seen in BLUE CAUSEWAY (Color Page 64). This painting shows the use of polymer emulsions as a stain on unstretched, unprimed raw canvas. If oil had been used the work would have a limited life because oil paint tends to rot raw canvas.

Miss Frankenthaler's application is a blending of drawing and painting, depth and transparency, foreground and background, paint and support, all becoming one with the other. There is no final varnish.

In contrast to the direction of Frankenthaler, where color becomes one with support, is POLYMER NO. 21-1958, Figure 28, by *Raymond Jonson,* Professor Emeritus, University of New

Mexico. In this work the paint is more stabilized in atmosphere and foreground-background relationships, although the handling is still fluid and spontaneous. The difference in effect is related to treating the support as a support rather than a part of the painting itself.

The support for POLYMER NO. 21-1958 was Masonite primed with several coats of synthetic gesso alternately rolled on in opposite directions with a felt paint roller, until the desired tooth was obtained. Then the marbled effect was achieved by pouring on water-diluted colors, allowing them to run together, and blowing the wet paint into configurations with the air stream from an air brush. Water was sprayed onto the colors to keep them workable for an extended period of time.

Artist and professor *Leon de Leeuw* exploits the area in between—in between staining, wash, tempera, and oil. His work can become one or all as his sensitivity dictates. But basically the effect is very much that of polymer used as a water-dispersed medium and employing the canvas as an integral part of the work.

IMPASSE, Figure 29, exhibits a veil of color that seems to float on the surface, held in ambiguous space by very fluid line. It is a controlled

Figure 28. POLYMER NO. 21-1958, 30 x 30 inches, by Raymond Johnson. Medium: LIQUITEX. (Courtesy: the artist.) The different esthetic directions allowed with fluid water-dispersed polymer color can be seen by comparing this painting to BLUE CAUSEWAY, Color Page 64, by Helen Frankenthaler.

Johnson's painting is achieved by flowing color ONTO a rigid ground support, while that of Frankenthaler allows color to become one with the raw support, flowing color INTO a porous, flexible surface. The nature of polymer emulsions allows a diversity of concepts.

Figure 29. IMPASSE, 34 x 50 inches, by Leon de Leeuw. Medium: LIQUITEX and AQUA-TEC. Although the ambiguous space is somewhat related to the color field directions in painting, a subjective approach is introduced here. (Photography by Charles Sauona.)

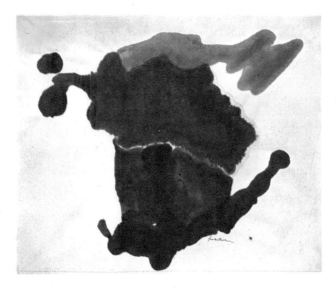

WATERWAYS, 72 x 60 inches, by Helen Lundeberg. Medium: NOVA COLOR, (Courtesy: the artist.) WATERWAYS was "drawn" on the canvas with quarter-inch masking tape, backed up with wider tape to prevent accidental overflow of color. The support is heavy cotton duck, stretched on a two-inch-deep box frame and primed with three coats of white. The priming, as well as the painting itself, continues around the edges of the deep stretcher, making framing unnecessary and unwanted. Painting techniques follow those described in the text. Lundeberg never stains or uses a spray unit because she prefers to control color, value gradation, transparencies in flat well-defined areas.

BLUE CAUSEWAY, 57 x 72 3/4 inches, by Helen Frankenthaler. Medium: AQUA-TEC. (Courtesy: the artist.) In Frankenthaler's staining technique on raw canvas, color becomes one with the support.

64

stain of color accomplished with washes, brush application, and rubbing. To retain the white or off-white of the canvas, de Leeuw often paints out areas of color with two coats of Titanium White and covers the white with gesso.

WOMAN, 1967, Figure 30, is more toward casein in effect but also contains washes of very thin color.

When de Leeuw first tried polymers he used them to duplicate oil techniques and was very much dissatisfied. Later he picked them up again, because he wanted a faster working material. After a month of experimentation he worked from oil-like applications to the uniquely polymer (and uniquely de Leeuw) approach.

As a teacher, as well as a practicing artist, de Leeuw encourages student exploration with polymers because they allow faster development and a directness not possible by traditional means. He exhibits at the Phoenix Gallery in New York.

Artist *Arthur Horsfall* has expanded his work to the field of fashion with his staining techniques. In 1968 the Winnipeg Art Gallery held a show entitled "Art in Fashion," which was devoted to Horsfall's painted fabrics. Instead of canvas, Horsfall applies polymer to a synthetic blend of viscose and cotton. Designer *Lois Juzak* then produces original dress concepts. (Figure 31.)

Artist Horsfall describes the process: "First the sizing is removed from the fabric with warm

Figure 30. WOMAN 1967, 50 x 48 inches, by Leon de Leeuw. Medium: LIQUITEX and AQUA-TEC. Linen canvas primed with polymer gesso is the support for de Leeuw's work. The washes and stains of original color, spontaneously applied, can be seen under a more casein-like overpainting. De Leeuw studied with Philip Guston, and in this painting he still retains some of the work "tracings" usually associated with the Abstract Expressionist school. (Photograph by Charles Sauona.)

Figure 31. PAINTED FABRICS by Arthur Horsfall. Dress styles by Lois Juzak. Medium: LIQUITEX. (Courtesy: Tajaylya Productions, Canada.) Paintings worked into dress designs are not unusual in the field of art today. Here the Color Field goes over to Pop.

water. The material here is viscose and cotton but other fabric can be used if the compatibility of the polymer with the fabric is tested first. Wet fabric is hung, stretched or stapled to a support, vertically. (If more control is desired the fabric can be stretched in space, horizontally, with ropes to the studio walls, and tilted and tied in successive color applications to achieve exact color flow.) The fabric is allowed to drip until the top is barely damp. Polymer emulsion colors are mixed with water to a cream-like consistency and applied with a brush. The tricky part is 'consistency.' If the paint is applied directly from the jar it will leave hard pieces of paint on the fabric; if the paint is applied too thinly then the color will be thin and could be washed out when the fabric is washed. The correct consistency makes the design washable and dry cleanable."

All this began when Juzak wanted something different to wear and asked Horsfall to paint her a dress. The result was Tajaylya Productions of Winnipeg, Manitoba, Canada.

66

6

Polymer Emulsions: The Painterly and Tactile Surface

Although polymer emulsion paints are water suspended and can be used specifically as water media, a no less honest and direct approach is to employ them for their painterly and tactile characteristics. The polymer tube colors are eminently suited for holding the brush and knife mark, as does an oil medium. They produce the most brilliant glazes of any media available. Impastos and textural characteristics are easily created with minimal work and drying time. And the mediums are excellent glues, allowing for permanent collage as well as three-dimensional and scuptural form. For those artists who prefer "the feel, look, and body of a paint" the polymer emulsion tube colors and mediums present limitless explorations.

As An Oil-Like Medium

Most tubed synthetics today have a viscous body like that of traditional oils. The characteristics of the material and its working qualities have been detailed in Chapter 2, *Tubed Polymer Emulsion Colors.* It bears repeating, however, that the artist must work much faster than in oil paint and that tubed polymers "feel" somewhat different than oils. Time must be spent in acquiring the touch of a new medium.

The approaches to painting are as varied as the artists who paint. Polymers are no exception. The following work may help the artist with his particular direction.

Direct Approach. LEONA, Figure 32, is a portrait of my younger daughter and illustrates the direct working qualities of polymer tube colors. The painting was done in two hours for two reasons: first, in work of this sort my habits are to paint as fast as possible to achieve a freshness and immediacy that would not be lost in overworking; second, because my daughter finds it impossible to sit for over five minutes at a time I *had* to work fast.

Figure 32. LEONA, 30 x 24 inches, by Russell Woody. Medium: LIQUITEX. A portrait finished in approximately two hours working time, using paint directly from the tube, applied rather heavily in most of the painting.

Figure 33. ORCHESTRA, 51 x 51 inches, by Russell Woody. Medium: LIQUITEX. (Collection: The Rev. and Mrs. John F. Salmon, Jr.) Tube color can be greatly thinned with water for wash and stain techniques, as was done in ORCHESTRA to establish the only color of the painting. Executed on raw canvas. To make raw canvas accept a wash it is best to wet it down and rub water into the whole canvas before the water-thinned polymer is applied. Heavy brush work over the stain can be seen in the detail (Figure 34).

Figure 34. Detail of ORCHESTRA, approximately 6 x 4 inches.

The painting was started with a vine charcoal sketch on a commercially primed polymer canvas. This quick sketch was fixed with a spray of half water and half gloss medium. My daughter took off and I established all color areas with washes of color, covering the whole canvas. All color throughout the painting was mixed on a glass palette.

The subject posed for another five minutes and the face and hands were painted in with undiluted tube color in a more or less impressionistic manner. Clothing and background were then brought to the same state of completeness. The work was allowed to dry completely, which took about thirty minutes.

My daughter was persuaded to sit still for another five minutes. Corrections were made in the the face, and the clothing folds were finished. (The drying time of polymer allows for almost immediate corrections.) The work was finished with glazes—lots of gloss medium and little color—to perfect skin tones and adjust background color. Polymer glazes can be much more brilliant than oil glazes because of the clarity of the medium. If oils had been used it would have taken weeks for drying time and overglazes. The painting was given two coats of gloss medium and hung the same day.

ORCHESTRA, Figure 33, is also done in a direct technique using washes of color allowed to show through the heavy, oil-like brush strokes. All the color was accomplished with very loose, water-dilute washes that were permitted to run and stain the raw canvas surface. The textural brush work is Mars Black and Titanium White. The texture of the raw canvas and the washes can be more clearly seen in the detail, Figure 34.

In 1959 *Milton Resnick* began a series of very large paintings in which he wanted to be able to work fast in order to achieve a sense of immediacy. He used polymer on paper and the result is difficult to distinguish from oil on canvas. In fact, these paintings were backed to canvas and have been listed and sold as oil on canvas at times. The result is seen in CAPRICORN, Figure 35.

Figure 35. CAPRICORN, 96 x 23 inches, by Milton Resnick. Medium: LIQUITEX. (Courtesy: Howard Wise Gallery, New York.) The technique here is direct, spontaneous, reactive, yet controlled. Very little paint is applied to the paper surface but the painting achieves a sensation of a heavy surface, at times almost projecting an impasto effect. Painting was done flat on the floor. To see the work vertically, a long stick was tacked to each end so it could be picked up and placed against the wall. When finished, it was glued to canvas with a synthetic glue (gel medium would work perfectly).

Figure 36. HEIR, painting in progress no. 1. Painting begins in abstract patterns over a textural ground of gel, modeling paste, and gesso. At this point, the paint on the canvas is mostly redissolvable tempera, which can be scrubbed out or isolated with polymer and painted over or into. When covered with sprays of polymer medium the tempera becomes waterproof and relatively permanent, if artists' quality tempera is used.

Re-working Dry Paint. Tom Vincent starts the majority of his easel paintings in an abstract manner, as seen in Figure 36. But the finished work, HEIR Figure 37, based on these abstract design principles, is figurative. His work has a high professional finish that is like oil painting but which also exploits the vibrancy and depth of polymer colors. Vincent's painting is unusual, technically, and would have been included in Chapter 7, "Mixed Media and Polymer," except that I defy anyone to look at his work and say it is polymer, not oil. For those who object to the idea that polymer cannot be reworked after it is dry, here is an outstanding artist's answer to the problem.

Vincent's support is usually linen canvas covered with two to three coats of polymer gesso. The linen is sometimes a better choice than cotton if a traditional oil quality is sought. Here, any resemblance to a traditional technique ends.

A textural surface is then built with a mixture of gel medium and modeling paste or the gel and paste is added to gesso and brushed on. (Half gel

and half paste should be used on a flexible support.) Concept begins at this point as the textural masses are pulled down and pushed around with paper. Paper is also pushed against wet areas and pulled off leaving textural marks and removing heavy pilings. Sometimes pieces of paper are left attached. After the textural design and build-up are to the artist's liking, the surface is allowed to dry.

At this point Vincent begins to paint, using a good grade of *water resoluble tempera paint*. The darker tones of tempera are applied and light areas are accomplished by rubbing off color with a wet sponge or brush. (See Figure 38.) In this manner Vincent continues to work, at times pulling off color areas down to the textural ground. With a tempera system such as this, areas can be corrected, moved, or wiped out entirely until the final design is achieved.

The artist says that two-thirds of the time the abstract forms dictate the final image. In other cases the image is pre-conceived, but worked up in the same technical manner.

Figure 37. HEIR, 57 x 48 inches, by Tom Vincent. Medium: LIQUITEX and tempera paint. If the artist wants the working qualities of polymer, the reworkability of oil or tempera, and the appearance of oil, he should follow the example of Tom Vincent.

Figure 38. HEIR, painting in progress no. 2. Here artist Vincent is shown cutting into an area, picking up the tempera paint with a wet brush. Compare the same area with HEIR, painting in progress no. 1, Figure 36. The photographs were taken in the artist's New Jersey studio.

Figure 39. UNTITLED PAINTING in progress, by Leon Golub. (Courtesy: the artist.) This shows the beginnings of a long build-up process by Golub. The artist's own description of his technique is given in the text. Finished paintings are tacked to a wall; they are stretched only when sold, or for a show. The paint gives with the canvas and will not develop cracks in stretching or if rolled for overseas shipment, unless the painting freezes.

Vincent then begins to use polymer emulsion colors along with the tempera, back and forth until the final work is completed. The painting is thoroughly sealed with spray coats of polymer matte varnish and matte medium mixed. Vincent sprays on about three very fine coats of his varnish, using a Mistral Miniature spray unit, which delivers a fine mist. To make sure the varnish will render permanent all tempera color not previously covered with polymer in the painting process, he scrubs the painting carefully with a wet sponge. If any color is picked up, more varnish is applied. (Also see Figures 49 and 50.)

Vincent is represented in many public and private collections, including those of the Kansas City Art Institute, the Springfield Museum of Fine Arts, the Atlanta Museum, Montclair Museum, Schering Corp. He has shown in the Museum of Modern Art, Corcoran Gallery, Pennsylvania Academy of Fine Arts.

Artist *Leon Golub's* technique is very personal, and symbolically related to his ideas, but his technical approach could be used by others. Basically, he applies raw, flat color directly from the jar (an exception to the general rule of tubed color in this chapter) and redissolves the polymer paint films with lacquer solvents.

He describes his process of working: "I start with small sketches, about nine by twelve inches, in pencil. These are transferred to raw, unstretched canvas by the grid system. The figures are given a coat of gesso—but not the background. There are two reasons for this: first, I like the look of the bare canvas, which produces a sort of universal space of anywhere, anytime; second, when I scrape down and dissolve the figures eventually the color becomes dull and the gesso helps keep a certain lightness, which I find preferable to the color over raw canvas.

"The figures are painted in a series of raw colors in staccato lines and strokes of color which produces a kind of irregular, terse rhythm. This is man in tension, the most extreme condition under which I can visualize contemporary man— moments of struggle, violence.

"The color (Red Oxide, black, white, pink, light blue) relates to a kind of organic, natural process of Classic Mediterranean or old fresco, or landscapes—a climatic kind of color. It does not have the look of a synthetic that polymer can possess; the flat, impersonal, somewhat artificial coloring of objects that is very attractive to many people.

"Then the painting is placed on the floor and saturated in lacquer solvents. As the paint film begins to be dissolved I cut into the sometimes fifteen layers of color with sculpture tools. I carve, erode the surface, strip it, reduce it. What I arrive at is a fragmentary kind of surface, as if these figures had been disintegrated over a long period of time.

"Paintings are reworked, rebuilt, and redissolved many times until I arrive at what I want. Once I stop working the surface, the disintegration stops. The volatile solvents evaporate out and the paint is permanent.

"In this way too, the paint becomes one with the canvas, burnt into it—but in a much different way than in Color Field painting where the paint on unsized canvas is absorbed almost instantly into the texture. Mine is burnt in; it does not float."

Figure 39 and COMBAT I, Figure 40, show Golub's technique, which is unique. The reader could adapt the solvent approaches to his own needs, however. The polymer emulsions are not damaged by being dissolved with lacquer thinner; they still retain permanency on the canvas. When using volatile solvents be sure proper ventilation is observed. Golub uses fans to remove the vapors.

The Tactile, Textural Painted Surface

All the paintings illustrated previously in this chapter have a textural surface to some extent caused by brush marks and oil-like paint manipulations, but they are not concerned *primarily* with a surface quality or contrasts of textural changes to make the painting work as the artist envisions. The following paintings are very much dependent on the development of tactile differences. The "feel" of the materials to the eye are paramount.

Carl Swallow states that in his personal development he has become increasingly interested in effects caused by subtle changes in color and in texture. Polymer paints are especially useful in achieving the effects, he says. This can be clearly seen in SPRING No. 2, Figure 41.

The work was done on cotton duck primed with a commercial acrylic housepaint. Sections of the canvas were masked with large pieces of heavy paper. Since the painting was executed in a horizontal position, the paper was simply held down

Figure 40. COMBAT (I), 96 x 72 inches, by Leon Golub. Medium: LIQUITEX. (Courtesy: the artist.) This completed work shows the results of reworking dried polymer paints with solvent.

with weights. Polymer color was thinned with gloss medium and applied with sponges and stencil brushes and spattered on by raking a putty knife over a paint-filled tooth brush.

Modeling paste can be used as a color in itself, something like a weak off-white, as well as a textural additive. The painting LURANAH, Figure 42, employs it in this manner. The work is a portrait of my oldest daughter and is accomplished in a completely different painting technique than LEONA, Figure 32.

The first steps were traditional. A Masonite panel was sanded and given four coats of gesso thinned slightly with water. A detailed drawing was done on the gesso with vine charcoal and fixed with a spray of gloss medium and water in a ratio of one to one. Spraying was done with a mouth atomizer. The color design of the whole painting was established with thin washes of color.

Then all colors were mixed to a thick consistency with modeling paste and polymer medium and applied with various bristle brushes. Although the painting was very heavy, no palette knives were used. All but the face was established completely

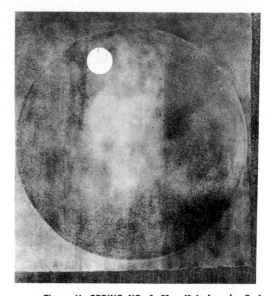

Figure 41. SPRING NO. 2, 50 x 48 inches, by Carl Swallow. Medium: AQUA-TEC and SEARS ACRYLIC LATEX. (Courtesy: the artist.) Although the colors are lyrical and intense, this painting depends on subtle textural changes for much of its impact, which is more evident in black-and-white reproduction than in color.

Figure 42. LURANAH, 24 x 33 inches, by Russell Woody. Medium: LIQUITEX. In direct contrast to LEONA, Figure 32, this portrait is based on a textural emphasis utilizing modeling paste as a paint as well as a means to heavy impasto.

Figure 43. POLARITIES I-A, 32½ x 41¾ inches, by George Chavatel. (Courtesy: the artist.) Several elements were employed to establish the artist's polarity concept in this painting: the flat paint area vs. the textural, opacity vs. translucency, and the dynamics of color opposites incremented with white areas employed positively and negatively.

in this manner. Glazes on the face and in a few adjacent areas completed the portrait.

To emphasize "an overall dynamic polarity of suitable oppositions, as in nature," *George Chavatel* used thin polymer contrasted with its opposite, the textural. The painting, POLARITIES I-A, Figure 43, was started with a highly dilute mixture of color and water to stain the gesso canvas and applied so the paint would dry "watery" in appearance. Then direct color was brushed on with a one-inch bright bristle brush. This was supplemented with impasto layers of modeling paste and gel "where a focus on planar transitions was to occur."

The final varnish was diluted gel medium, lightly applied. If the artist wants tubed medium as opposed to gloss medium in jars, gel medium is the answer, and as in this case, it can be thinned with water to a flowing consistency.

Textural Additives

Almost any granular, textural material can be combined with polymer emulsion mediums and paints since the materials are excellent binders. If the additive is absorbent then medium (gel is best) should be used as well as paint to insure the flexibility of the mixture on anything but a rigid panel.

Artist *Raymond Jonson* often uses such textural additives as Plexiglas, clean sawdust, white sand, marble dust, ripped wood shavings, etc. A detail of his POLYMER NO. 6-1963, Color Page 82, shows two different additive techniques in contrast with a flatly painted surface. The "top" upside down "Y" linear structure is composed of Korena wood-dust and shavings, gloss medium, and bright red polymer. The mixture was applied with a spoon and tweezers. The black line is sand mixed with paint and medium.

A very coarse bird gravel was used for the heavy textural areas in MATADOR, Figure 44. It was mixed with gel medium and applied with a painting knife. Line was drawn into heavy tube color with the handle of the brush. Much of the color in this painting is raw pigment sifted onto wet medium. The pigment is somewhat lumpy, and when covered with several spray coats of gloss medium it becomes permanently bound into the plastic films and creates more texture. Large sticks of vine charcoal were used to draw over this very rough surface. In doing so the charcoal broke off in fine particles and these, too, were sealed into the paint surface with sprays of medium.

To insure that all these additive materials would not release from the painting, six coats of undiluted gloss medium were carefully brushed over the surface.

Artist *Toby Joysmith* has used commercial brands of polymer, which are employed as industrial glues and sealers. He has the background and experience to determine which of the industrial synthetics suit his purpose. As a teacher he initiated courses on synthetics at the University of the Americas in Mexico City.

Joysmith uses Masonite as a support and gives it a heavy coat of the acrylic sealer; he paints on either the smooth or the rough side, depending on the adhesive qualities he needs. He applies at least four coats of acrylic emulsion white as a ground, and, if he decides to paint on the rough side, he adds sifted, powdered pumice stone to the last two coats.

Joysmith describes his technique as it applies to PYRAMID I, Figure 45: "I tend to draw with a point into a wet medium mixture which is spread on the support. At times I have used wool yarn dipped in the emulsion to create these structure lines (see the left side and bottom of the pyramid).

"The mixtures I use to obtain textures vary in composition but are made basically with *Resistol 850* (or a polymer gloss medium), plaster, powdered pumice stone and water. If I want a rougher texture I add sawdust or even powdered

cork. For very fine textures I sift pumice through a cloth. The textures are built up with a knife or the fingers, or else a flat board is dragged across the surface.

"If the painting begins to go wrong I attack it with a stone chisel and hammer and obliterate most of the texture. This generally gives a good base for future operations.

"When the mixture is dry (in about two or three hours, depending on its thickness), I begin to adjust the values in each form by using scumbles or glazes—generally both. I use many glazes, building hot on cold, and never allow any dead color to stand which has not been modified by a glaze."

(See also Figure 65 in Chapter 8, "Mural Painting.")

Collage

Collage means "pasting," and that is literally what is done in a true collage approach. Today very few works are entirely collage—they usually combine all techniques.

Collage had its roots in Cubism, when textures or objects were duplicated or suggested by gluing bits of the objects, or things that resembled them, onto the canvas. In its present development it holds its own as a fine arts technique and is employed in all esthetic directions.

Acrylic polymer emulsion mediums are excellent glues for bonding almost any material to the painting support. If used properly they protect and seal the collage elements. All materials should be covered completely with medium, front and back (and sides, if necessary) for correct results.

(See also *Comparison of Polymer Emulsion Types,* Chapter 1, and *Gloss Medium, Matte Medium, Matte Varnish,* and *Gel Medium,* Chapter 2.)

George Chavatel often uses collage elements in his work. KINETICISM V-A, Figure 46, illustrates the pure collage technique. The support was Upsom board, which had been given two moderately diluted coatings of gesso. Corrugated cardboard, the only material used in this work, was

Figure 44. MATADOR, 18 x 24 inches, by Russell Woody. Medium: LIQUITEX. Although the support for this painting is canvas, the heavy textural materials used will not crack or flake off because copious quantities of gel and gloss medium were used to adhere and coat the additives.

Figure 45. PYRAMID I, 96 x 122 cms., by Toby Joysmith. Medium: RESISTOL 850. Joysmith thinks one of the best points of polymer is the clarity and intensity of glazes as used here over textural surfaces built of balsa wood, yarn, plaster, and powdered pumice stone. The color is very somber and earthy, with an orange accent. The black at bottom right was glazed with hot yellow and Ochre to give a rusty effect.

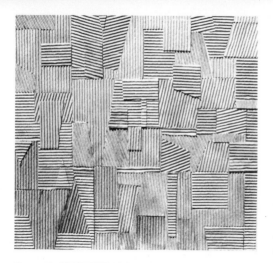

Figure 46. KINETICISM V-A, 25 1/2 x 25 1/2 inches, by George Chavatel. Medium: LIQUITEX. (Courtesy: the artist.) This is a true collage, using polymer gloss medium as the binder and varnish.

pre-cut and coated with gloss medium. The support was also liberally brushed with gloss medium and the design components were glued on. After all the cardboard was affixed, the whole surface was given two applications of thinned gloss medium to act as a varnish.

The artist says, "My intention was to develop a greater understanding about the conditions of light, so much a factor in how one views artistic form. At the same time I wanted to incorporate the effects of light on a two-dimensional surface into a context based on continuity. Obviously, it was intended to develop dynamic relationships between components which 'had a life of their own' outside of any reliance on representational equivalency."

Another collage by Chavatel elaborates the variety of materials that can be attached to the working surface. ONENESS, Figure 47, uses cut wood and paper, cloth of various types (including an

Figure 47. ONENESS (Transition xxxv-B), 16 x 24 inches, by George Chavatel. Medium: LIQUITEX. Three-dimensional collage elements here produce "wells" between the objects, making color difficult to apply, but allowing for ease in achieving a variegated coloration via the recessed areas and the projecting ones. Color was dry-brushed over the textural elements and the effect of its texture was enhanced with gel glazes.

old pair of shorts) and metals (mostly aluminum). The collage support is untempered Masonite primed with polymer gesso. The board was braced with one- by two-inch strips of fir around the back perimeter and through the center. All objects were adhered with polymer gesso, which Chavatel often uses as a glue, and coated with gesso after they were placed.

Dry brush scumbling of color was done over the textural surface. Glazes made with one part color to six parts gel medium were brushed over the dry-brushed color.

In POLYMER NO. 45-1962, Figure 48, *Raymond Jonson* used paint skins that had dried inside the polymer jars. These plastic films, usually discarded by artists, were pulled from the bottom of the jars and affixed to paper that had been sprayed with tones of yellow.

Pieces of polymer were also prepared for this painting by pouring acrylic paint onto a clean sheet of glass. After several hours these poured shapes were dry; they were then soaked with water and carefully removed from the glass. Paint skins on glass will release within fifteen minutes to an hour, depending on the thickness of the dry paint and how wet it is kept. In this manner the artist can paint or pour his own collage elements, developing his own color and texture. The paint skins are adhered to the support with gloss medium. (See Figure 4, Chapter 3.)

Taking this technique one step further, the artist can paint his whole painting on glass and remove it, when dry, by soaking the entire painting in water. If this is done the paint must be relatively thick, for thin films may rip when pulled from the glass. It is best to give the whole glass two to four coats of gloss medium first, to obtain a better release and prevent ripping. To assure an easier start in pulling the painting, a cellophane tape can be attached to the edges of the glass and painted over.

A painting removed from glass in this manner is really a paint skin. It can be attached to any surface with gloss medium, or a heavy painting can be stretched on stretcher strips—no canvas,

Figure 48. POLYMER NO. 45-1962, 32 1/4 x 21 1/2 inches, by Raymond Jonson. Medium: LIQUITEX. (Courtesy: the artist.) The translucent forms at the lower left and the circular forms that run between the two large top and bottom shapes are polymer paint films stripped from the bottoms of the jars in which the paint is sold. The artist created similar films for the large shapes by pouring color on glass. To achieve the runs, he tilted the glass; to produce the rings, he pulled wet paint out and looped it around with a stick. (See Figure 4, Chapter 3.)

Figure 49. THE MIND'S EYE, 44 x 55 inches, by Tom Vincent. Medium: LIQUITEX and tempera paint. (Courtesy: the artist.) Images from magazines and newspapers as well as direct drawing and painting are used in this multiple collage.

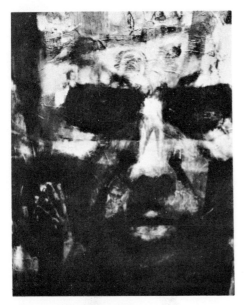

Figure 50. Detail of THE MIND'S EYE.

paper, or support is needed, just pure paint all the way through. Lights can be placed behind the work. If it is very transparently done (with the addition of medium), you can see through the paint and several paintings can be placed one behind the other and lighted for very unusual effects. The possibilities for using polymer in this manner are endless.

Transfers of printed photographs or reproductions can be accomplished in a similar technique: A reproduction from a newspaper or magazine is given three or more coats of gloss medium. When dry, it is soaked in water until the uncoated back of the paper becomes soggy. The paper can then be carefully pulled off, leaving the printing inks in the polymer; after the polymer transfer is dry it will usually be translucent because of the nature of printing inks. It can be adhered to any surface with gloss medium.

The realistic image can also be enhanced by polymer collage as in *Tom Vincent's* THE MIND'S EYE, Figure 49. This work is about two-thirds drawing and painting and one-third collage. The support is linen canvas primed with polymer gesso. Over this, a very realistic self portrait was drawn and worked up with tones of polymer color.

The portrait was varnished with matte varnish and work continued with water resoluble tempera paints. This enabled the artist to rework color areas and designs by thinning and washing out dry tempera areas with water.

Matte varnish in a spray application was again used to isolate and waterproof the tempera colors. At this point collage figures and objects cut from mass media sources were introduced. Both the surface of the painting and the backs of the collage subjects were painted with medium, then stuck together.

Some of the reproductions dried with a wrinkled texture that fascinated the artist. So, after coating the collage elements with more medium, the texture was increased with overlays of transparent tissue paper. The tissue was then soaked with medium, and varnished with medium when dry.

Not all the small figures throughout THE MIND'S EYE are collage. Some are drawings and paintings. For example, the laughing face on the artist's forehead is a collage reproduction, while the white-line reclining figure to the right of the chin is a drawing that duplicates a design Vincent did for Steuben glass. (See Figure 50.)

Toward the Sculptural

It can no longer be said that a work is a painting, as distinguished from sculpture. The artist works in between these areas many times. The shaped canvas as seen in STEEPLE CHASE (Color Page 61) is not a painting in the traditional sense. Neither is the heavy textural work of the Spanish school, nor hung minimal sculpture-painting. New materials such as polymer emulsions lead the artist into these non-categories.

My own work began with tactile surfaces, which started to become sculptural in nature when I wanted to control the canvas support as well as the paint and aggregate materials applied to it. Figure 51, MAGIC SUBSTANCE, is a painting that attempts to do so.

The polymer-primed canvas was given three coats of flat Mars Black jar color. Heavy textural paint, composed of Mars Black mixed with a

talcum-powder-like additive called Celite, was applied with brush and painting knives. Since no medium was mixed with the paint and Celite, the surface cracked. The more Celite incorporated into the paint, the more cracking develops. It can be controlled with a little practice.

Shapes were then cut out of the center of the figure with a matte knife, stuffed with more canvas and shaped. In order to retain its configurations, the canvas was given about six coats of a mixture of gel medium, Mars Black, and modeling paste in a one to one to one ratio by volume. This gave

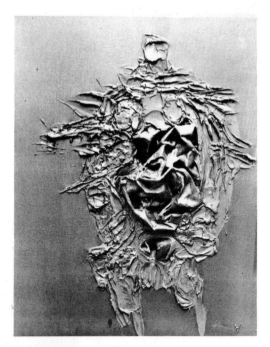

Figure 51. MAGIC SUBSTANCE, 34 x 24 inches, by Russell Woody. Medium: LIQUITEX. This entirely black painting attempts to control the canvas as well as the paint by cutting, shaping, and solidifying the canvas with polymer emulsion materials.

RED BALL. 30 x 24 inches, by Russell Woody. Medium: LIQUITEX. (Collection: The Rev. Canon Walter D. Dennis.) The use here of flat drawing, flat painting, sculptural form, and mixed fluorescent color is entirely dependent on the polymer mediums for permanency and workability. Materials employed in this manner can help express concretely a feeling about idea and subject almost impossible to achieve with traditional media and concept.

SIXTH TO NINTH HOUR, NO. 12, 40 x 30 inches, by Russell Woody. Medium: LIQUITEX. (Collection: Schering Corporation.) This three-dimensional painting is reproduced in color to show the different effects black-on-black can take in a painting-sculpture technique.

Detail of POLYMER NO. 6-1963, about 12 x 10 inches, by Raymond Jonson. Medium: LIQUITEX. (Courtesy: the artist.) The hard edge of the textural design shows the control possible in this technique, as described under Textural Additives.

the canvas body and texture as well as gluing it permanently in place. Gloss medium was painted over the figure in spots to vary the intensity and surface quality of the black.

SIXTH TO NINTH HOUR, NO. 12, Color Page 82, projects the paint materials from the canvas surface into sculptural space. The canvas was coated with black, and a sheet of hardboard, also painted black, was nailed to the stretcher strips at the back of the canvas. Since the canvas was to be cut, the hardboard would give a second surface plane to the painting.

A figure was painted and modeled with knives on a wax-paper-covered palette. Gel medium, modeling paste, black tube color, and Shreddi-Mix papier-mâché were used to obtain a mixture that would solidify into a permanent, quite light weight, dry form. These materials require about a day to dry thoroughly and can be removed from the wax paper without problems.

To attach the sculptural paint form, short dowel rods were inserted into the form and glued with gel. Then the rods were pushed through holes cut into the canvas and sunk into previously drilled holes in the hardboard, and again glued with gel.

To complete the painting, a matte knife was used to cut the shapes out of the first plane of the painting.

RED BALL, Color Page 82, uses the same technique in the projections but also incorporates fluorescent pigment as well as a drawing. The drawing was done first on a gesso canvas, using black and sepia conté crayon and vine charcoal. This was sealed with half gloss medium and half water sprayed from a Jet Pak. The black ground was brushed on with undiluted jar color, so there would be slight brush strokes evident. Sculptural forms were attached, then the ball was covered with a paint made by mixing fluorescent red-orange with gel medium.

The extension of this technical and esthetic approach is a free-standing and free-hanging painting. Figure 52, SIXTH TO NINTH HOUR, NO. 20, illustrates the concept. The free-standing canvas is actually two canvases back to back, with

Figure 52. SIXTH TO NINTH HOUR, NO. 20, 23 x 12 x 10 inches, by Russell Woody. Medium: LIQUITEX. With the use of polymer mediums, multiple canvases, and additive materials, the artist is free to follow ,form and extend the function of the painting. The work is painterly in concept, even in the sculptural form built with brushes and painting knives. Yet the work is free to function in space.

holes cut into each canvas to reveal fluorescent paint on the back-up canvas.

Carl Swallow's work adheres more to the Hard Edge or Minimal point of departure. The basic shape of UNTITLED SCULPTURE was cut from a large piece of *Styrofoam* with a hand saw. The surface was covered and filled with modeling paste to obtain a smooth, firm, permanent ground for painting. Areas were masked with tape and all color was applied in a spatter technique by scraping a putty knife across a paint-filled tooth brush. The paint was mixed with matte medium and water to achieve a proper viscosity for this type of application. (See Figure 53.)

Swallow works on the West Coast and has exhibited widely in Mexico and California. His gallery is the Los Angeles Art Association.

Artist *Marisol Escobar* states she is not too interested in paint as a direction, but uses polymer emulsions in her unique constructions because of its fast drying quality. The concept of the work, she says, directs the color, handling, and choice of media, as seen in THE DEALERS, Figure 54.

Figure 54. THE DEALERS, 74 x 74 x 47 inches, by Marisol. Medium: AQUA-TEC and mixed media. (Courtesy: Sidney Janis Gallery, New York; photograph by Geoffrey Clements.) Marisol uses polymer emulsion colors for pragmatic reasons: it works and dries fast, is permanent, and the colors are more brilliant. In this multi-piece work all paint is polymer. There is also drawing sealed with plastic sprays, and sculpture molds of the artist's face.

Figure 53. UNTITLED SCULPTURE, 33 1/2 x 16 x 4 inches, by Carl Swallow. Medium: LIQUITEX. (Courtesy: the artist.) Here the Hard Edge approach is converted to sculptural form with polymer modeling paste and paint over STYROFOAM.

7

Mixed Media and Polymer

All water-soluble materials, such as watercolor, tempera, and casein paints, may be mixed with polymer emulsion mediums and color for special effects and techniques. Also various types of graphic media may be used in conjunction with polymers.

While polymer emulsions should never be mixed with oil paints, the two media can be combined in painting. Polymers make good underpainting and ground materials for oils, and the oil paint can be applied over the polymer as soon as it is dry to the touch. Many artists have started to use polymer paints as fast-drying underpaint media and finish with washes and glazes of oil.

This chapter will illustrate some of the various approaches that employ additive materials for their visual impact. The use of tempera paints with polymer has been illustrated with the work of Tom Vincent. (See HEIR, Figure 37, Chapter 6, and THE AGES OF MEDICINE, Figure 63, Chapter 8.)

Figure 55, study for SLEEPING CHILD, shows how ink can be combined with the material. A small piece of linen canvas was stretched and given four coats of heavily brushed on gesso. The figure and the related forms were drawn over this slightly textural ground with India Ink. A thin white glaze was brushed over the entire drawing to reduce the intensity of the black line. Twenty or more thin glazes followed, using gloss medium and very little color. A final varnish of one part matte varnish and five parts gloss protected portions of gesso at the sides of the study, left uncovered with glazes.

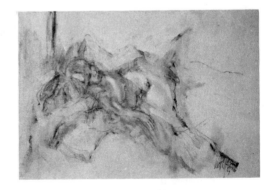

Figure 55. Study for SLEEPING CHILD, 16 x 24 inches, by Russell Woody. Media: LIQUITEX and India Ink. Basically a drawing on canvas, this study was modified with multiple glazing.

Figure 56. LANDSCAPE 1964, by Allan D'Arcangelo. Media: LIQUITEX, charcoal, pencil, and collage. (Courtesy: the artist and Fischbach Gallery; photograph by Eric Pollitzer. Collection: Rodrigo Moynihan.) The whole effect of LANDSCAPE is based on the ability of polymer emulsions to incorporate graphic media permanently into the working technique.

Graphic materials as well as a small piece of collage gives LANDSCAPE, Figure 56, by *Allan D'Arcangelo* its unusual quality of image. The support for the painting was Masonite over which canvas was adhered with a commercial polymer emulsion glue. The canvas, as well as the hardboard, was liberally coated with the glue and the canvas was rolled onto the board from the center outward to prevent air bubbles. The edges were pulled and tacked down when the canvas started to set up and shrink.

The canvas was primed with gesso and two coats of Titanium White. A post card was glued to the center of the canvas with medium and its elements were expanded. Top left shows charcoal work; the bottom square is pencil drawing. These were fixed, and then flat areas of polymer paint completed the work.

WOMAN S, Figure 57, demonstrates graphic material used as paint. Figure and background were drawn on a gesso canvas with charcoal and multicolor pastels. Polymer gloss medium and water (two-thirds water, one-third medium) was then brushed over and into the drawing, blending the pastels and making a paint out of them. Some line areas were scrubbed into a wash while others were just barely covered, preserving their linear quality. A whole painting could be done in this technique without the addition of paint. But in this case Titanium White was applied straight from the tube as impasto. The work was varnished with two coats of gloss medium to insure that the pastels would remain waterproof.

James Brooks has used various media in his paintings, including oils, polymer emulsions, polymer solutions, charcoal, pastels, and textural additives. "The eye," he says, "may be sensitive to one-hundredth of an inch difference in the depth of paint surface, and therefore should react to the quality of depth presented by each medium."

Brooks, as in COOBA, Figure 58, builds up a painting with combinations of thin washes and opaque paints. He rubs on thin tints and tones of polymer with a rag or paper. Areas of liquid paint are applied and blotted off with an absorbent paper, as can be clearly seen in the painting's circular forms.

If more viscous paint is desired he sometimes adds asbestine to the colors (asbestine tints the colors slightly, but not appreciably). The painting gradually builds, and when completed it has a depth and luminosity and a translucent quality that are the very touchstones of the polymer emulsions. However, the treatment of line in COOBA was done with *Magna,* an acrylic polymer solution paint, because Brooks could not achieve the effect he wanted with acrylic emulsion paint.

In MOONBIRTH, Figure 59, *Toby Joysmith* shows the use of polymer emulsion as an underpaint and textural buildup for oil glazes. The flat areas were executed in many layers of thinly applied polymer. Ground pumice mixed with polymer white was used for the impasto moon form.

Figure 57. WOMAN S, 24 x 48 inches, by Russell Woody. Media: LIQUITEX, charcoal and pastel. Polymer medium was used to make a paint of charcoal and pastel. Gloss medium over the graphic color intensifies the pigment, rendering it much more brilliant than in its normal state.

Figure 58. COOBA, 80 x 74 inches, by James Brooks. Media: LIQUITEX, MAGNA over DUTCH BOY latex white. Primed with DUTCH BOY latex (an acrylic emulsion) and painted mainly with LIQUITEX (an acrylic polymer emulsion), the line here was accomplished with MAGNA (an acrylic polymer solution) squeezed directly from the tube. (All the polymers are compatible as they are all acrylic. The artist found in MAGNA a response he could not obtain with the emulsion form of acrylic.)

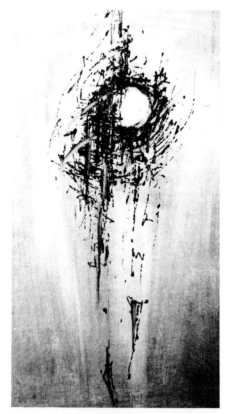

Figure 59. MOONBIRTH, 125 x 55 centimeters, by Toby Joysmith. Media: POLITEC, oil and pumice. (Collection: Dr. and Mrs. Robert Young.) The "written" lines as well as the glazes in the painting are oils over polymer.

Figure 60. RIVULETO, 52 x 36 inches, by Syd Solomon. Media: LIQUITEX and oil paint. (Courtesy: the artist. Photograph by John F. Waggaman.) The painting is on a polymer gesso primed linen canvas. Underpainting proceeded directly with polymer colors. Thin oil-paint glazes were applied over this. When the oil glaze was partially dry, it was wiped or lightly rubbed with a cloth to remove excess oil. Then a second (or double) glaze, composed of water-thinned emulsion and color, was applied. The water-based glazes over the dry oil glazes produced a CRAZE—a fine alligator type separation, which effects a thin textural surface. This can be seen especially in the right and bottom portions of RIVULETO.

The line, however, was black oil paint given body by the addition of an oil varnish and squeezed from a fine-tipped plastic sauce-bottle. The painting was finished with glazes of oil colors, which were allowed to partially dry and then wiped with a cloth. The layers of acrylic emulsion plus the thin oils result in a great depth and translucency.

Syd Solomon uses oils and polymer emulsions in combination. I do not recommend the process as a standard practice but if the artist is sure of his techniques, as Solomon is, then it can be accomplished. Solomon has worked with synthetics since 1940 and knows what can and cannot be done in his own approach.

Basically, the idea is to reduce the amount of linseed oil in the oil paints to a minimum, so that the polymer will adhere when applied over the oil. Solomon uses a kind of reconstituted oil, at times. Oil paints are thinned with mineral spirits and brushed over absorbent paper. When most of the linseed oil has been absorbed, the paint is reactivated with mineral spirits and wiped over the painting in a glazing method. He then paints with polymer over this fast drying oil.

In RIVULETO, Figure 60, a double glaze of oil under polymer was employed to produce a texturing effect specifically desired in this case. But this is what might happen in most cases if the artist does not have complete control.

8

Mural Painting

Mural decoration can be easily accomplished with the polymer emulsions. They do not require new approaches or techniques. The artist can paint as he has painted, carry all his personal ways of working with polymers to the execution of the mural. Techniques described in the preceding chapters of this book apply to mural painting as well as easel painting. There are no limitations.

Emulsion paints can be painted directly over mural grounds such as concrete, plaster, and even concrete block. The only requirement is that the wall surface be free of loose particles. The paints do not sink in, but stay on the surface of all porous materials with remarkable adhesion An exception to this is "cement paint" or waterproofing. If this has been applied to a wall surface then any paint put over it will peel in a few years. Cement *paint* is not the same thing as cement or plaster.

For best results the wall should be given a good coat of polymer gesso. This insures a smooth flow of paint and prevents water from being absorbed out of the paint by the porous wall surface so fast that painting becomes difficult.

The best support for mural painting is a false wall erected in front of an existing wall. The use of a false wall eliminates the dangers inherent in the expansion and contraction of a plaster wall. It also protects against cracking or peeling of plaster and damage to masonry walls by water seepage from behind.

Untempered or thoroughly sanded tempered Masonite panels have proved most useful as false walls. They should be fastened securely to a wood frame backing with the Masonite glued to cross bracings at least every twenty-four inches, using top grade animal furniture glue. The backs of these should be sealed with an acrylic resin or acrylic lacquer to prevent warping. Large murals may need several sheets of Masonite. If so, a space of one-eighth to one-quarter inch should be left between panels when putting them together. A piece of linen spanning this gap and glued to the Masonite with medium keeps the wall continuous. If there are bumps or lines where butting occurs, five or six coats of gesso or Titanium White as a ground will obliterate them. If a canvas support is desired, it can be glued to the Masonite with gel medium as described under *Supports,* Chapter 3.

After a mural is completed, a coating of matte varnish or several coats of gloss medium should be applied to protect the paint. If this is done most polymer murals can withstand public comment for quite a while—the public comment can be cleaned off with soap, water, and a scrub brush.

There is no paint available today that will withstand outside weathering conditions over a long period of time. The polymers are better than other artists' materials available, but only colored ceramics will be lasting enough for a *permanent* outdoor mural. All organic materials, as well as inorganic matter, are eventually affected by the sun and the constant weathering by the elements.

Outside murals in polymer can be given longer life by using several good coats of medium as protection. The more opaque pigments should be selected as they help screen the fading effects of ultra violet light from the sun. No water should be mixed with the colors, only medium. The artist should use straight color and do as little mixing of colors as possible. These rules, if followed, will assure the survival of the outdoor mural for several years, at least.

The *Liquitex* manufacturer has had a small test mural facing south and exposed to all weather conditions, including rain and snow, for over ten years. It was not given a coat of medium as protection. In three years it began to show the eroding effects of weather—the more transparent passages weathering faster due to greater penetration of the paint film by ultraviolet rays. A traditional paint would have vanished long before under such abuse.

A mural I painted in Mexico at the ten-thousand-feet level is still in good condition after weathering for eight years. It had several protective coatings of gloss medium.

The work of *Thomas Hart Benton* is especially suited to mural painting. INDEPENDENCE AND THE OPENING OF THE WEST, Figure 61, painted for the Harry S. Truman Library in Independence, Missouri, is an example. Its unique appearance results from Benton's strongly three-di-

Figure 61. INDEPENDENCE AND THE OPENING OF THE WEST, mural, 19 x 37 feet, by Thomas Hart Benton. Medium: LIQUITEX. (Courtesy: Harry S. Truman Library.) This is one of the first large murals to be done with polymer emulsions. Since the mural faces large windows, reflections from these could have destroyed the effectiveness of the work. Therefore, the mural was given a final matte varnish. As can be seen in the reproduction, no reflection is evident on the mural, although there are glares on the surface of the floor and the marble wall.

large work, Benton painted the upper area in a relatively free and broad manner, using large bristle brushes, and developed the lower areas at eye level with finely detailed work accomplished with small sable brushes. (See Figure 62.)

Tom Vincent's mural, THE AGES OF MEDI-CINE, stresses a more tactile approach to the paint surface. Vincent uses tempera paints as well as polymer emulsion so that areas can be reworked as described in Chapter 6, HEIR, Figure 36. The mural was commissioned by The Schering Corporation and depicts the development of medicine from Egyptian times to the present. The artist spent many months in the research and the design of the mural, even to the point of constructing a scale model of the room in which the mural was to be placed; the room being designed around the work.

Figure 63 shows an installation view of THE AGES OF MEDICINE. The painting itself was done in the artist's studio; when finished, it was rolled, carried to its permanent location, and then stretched on professionally built, extra heavy stretchers. The wall is a false one, erected for the painting. A detail of a center figure is reproduced on Color Page 49. This shows the painter's technique to better advantage.

THE ELEMENTS, Figure 64, is an example of an abstract mural done with polymer emulsion paints. The work, by *Leo Manso,* was painted on half-inch-thick Masonite panels. Each of the three panels was cradled with one- by three-inch pine strips attached to the panel with a polymer glue, under pressure. A three-coat ground of gesso was applied, each coat sanded smooth.

The artist describes his work: "The mural evolved organically using polymer emulsion colors from thin to thick, or heavy, painting. There was no planning of the artistic concept; rather, the theme was a continuation of a body of work concerning light, erosion, movement, earth.

"A panel was started, carried to a middle stage of finish, then set aside. A second panel was begun and brought to a higher level of finish. The first panel was placed in the central position, and the

Figure 62. Detail of INDEPENDENCE AND THE OPENING OF THE WEST. This detail of the top center portion of Benton's mural shows the broad handling the artist used in the upper sections as opposed to the fine detail at eye-level.

mensional style of painting in combination with the brilliant and luminous quality of the plastic medium. Benton made many studies and sketches before starting the work, and he even constructed a three-dimensional clay model in high detail, which he could study for light and shadow values in the manner of Tintoretto.

The 945-square-foot model was painted on heavy Belgian linen attached with polyester adhesive to a plaster wall reinforced with steel mesh. Six coats of full strength gesso were used as ground. Benton used a standard tempera technique in executing the mural. He transferred a cartoon to the squared-off canvas in the traditional manner. Over this pencil design, he applied the polymer colors directly.

In order to aid the eye of the viewer on such a

second one placed to the left. These were further integrated. The last panel was resolved rather fully and placed to the right.

"All three panels were then worked on all over to bring the work into a conceptual and artistic unity.

"Technically, painting was begun with the panels placed flat on waist-high stools. This made for the greatest freedom in painting, since it permitted walking around the work in any direction. The panels were later laid against the wall so they could be seen in a vertical position.

Figure 63. THE AGES OF MEDICINE, 78 x 246 inches, by Tom Vincent. (Installation view.) Medium: LIQUITEX and tempera paint. (Collection: Schering Corporation.) Due to the permanency and flexibility of polymer emulsions this mural was painted in the studio, rolled, then taken to its permanent location and stretched there. The work is done in muted blues, greens, and earth colors for the most part. Vincent's painterly technique is clearly evident in the detail reproduced on Color Page 49.

Figure 64. THE ELEMENTS, 76 x 144 inches, by Leo Manso. (Composed of three panels, each 48 x 76 inches.) Medium: LIQUITEX. (Collection: Lincoln Public Library, Lincoln, Nebraska.) The surfaces of this mural range from transparent and luminous areas to dense, opaque, and heavily textured effects. The ability to paint out areas with gesso and repaint in a short time enabled the artist to achieve his organic approach to painting more effectively.

"Transparent washes of polymer color, water, and matte medium started the painting. Corrections, or deletions, were made with gesso over unsatisfactory areas. The painting was then built, in part, into thick areas, with modeling paste used for impasto and color and medium added. Sometimes indications drawn in pastel colors were sprayed with the matte medium to bind them. When more luminosity was desired, gesso with binder was applied over an area, and glazes of transparent color laid over the clear underpainted white.

"When the panels were finished they were locked into position with metal straps screwed into the back of the wood cradling."

Manso, who works and teaches in Provincetown, Massachusetts, and New York City, was one of the first artist-teachers to investigate the whole range of plastic media in his own work and instruct his students in these techniques.

Three-dimensional, bas relief, or heavily textured surfaces can be accomplished with polymer emulsions and additive materials in the mural. *Toby Joysmith's* mural, commissioned by the Women's Hospital in Mexico, is a good example. There were five panels in the series, one of which is reproduced here (Figure 65).

A variety of tactile surfaces typify much of Joysmith's work. In this mural balsa wood strips, pumice stone, sawdust, plaster, and wool yarn formed the bases of various areas. These materials were either mixed with plastic emulsion (this was true of the plaster, sawdust, and pumice) or attached with the vehicle (as were the balsa and yarn).

Figure 65. MOTHER AND CHILD. Panel I of the five-panel mural MOTHERHOOD, by Toby Joysmith. Each panel measures 1 meter, 60 centimeters x 2 meters. Medium: Acrylic emulsion mixed with textural additives and pigment. (Courtesy: the artist.) These panels were built with additive materials, modelled with painting knives and the fingers, and heavily glazed. Lines were incised and built with yarn and balsa wood. The predominant colors are earth pigments with sharp accents of greenish blue and orange. They were painted flat, on a large table.

9

Collagraphy and other Printing Techniques

Collagraphy

Print making is a major form of artistic expression today and Collagraphy is fast becoming a dominant technical approach to this field. The name is descriptive of the process: Collagraphy is a collage build up of a printing surface. The plate is inked, wiped, and printed in a manner similar to an etching plate.

A collagraph plate is developed from a more painterly point of view than the usual linear approach to plate making. The artist's ideas are more immediately expressed because of the elimination of the usual multiple block-outs and multiple acid baths required in the traditional etching or aquatint processes.

Collagraphy can produce the visual effects of etching, aquatint, or mezzotint, as well as having its own, almost innumerable, visual possibilities. All this can be accomplished without the complicated, time consuming, hazardous, and expensive processes usually associated with plate making. In fact, this is the first time that professional printing results can be accomplished in either the public school room or the smallest studio, as well as in the best equipped college graphics department, with very little money or time expended.

Glen Alps, Professor of Art at the University of Washington, has probably done more than any other artist to give the collagraphic process impetus. He introduced the collagraph to his classes in 1965 and has taught the process as guest professor

and lecturer at many leading colleges and universities throughout the United States and Canada.

Alps states: "Collagraphy is a building-up process, a positive rather than a negative action. It is a liberating force for the printmaker. It can be a very direct confrontation with the plate as well as being a very deliberate, carefully planned, or even geometrically achieved work.

"The collagraph developed out of an inner urge to liberate the printmaker from long arduous hours of plate development at a time when much of our present living, working, creating is a *now* thing. This time element in developing a plate is a tremendous factor in the creation of an idea. An idea can be completed on a collagraph plate very quickly by using what I call *painting* or build-up techniques. So the collagraph came into being as a contemporary necessity and is being used today as such by artists in all parts of the world."

The collagraph is basically produced by adhering textural materials to a base of cardboard or hardboard with polymer emulsions. All types of images can be formed by the use of cloth, paper, cardboard, sand, powdered carborundum, ground walnut shells, sawdust, wood chips, plastic wood, polymer modeling paste, etc. The list is infinite. The additives can be imbedded in polymer without a final coat of polymer, if ink absorbent surfaces are desired, or coated with polymer to give a non-absorbent quality for a cleaner wiping of the ink.

The intaglio (a kind of reverse relief) surface thus formed can be carved or dug into at times, or can be contrasted or combined with a relief achieved by adhering areas of cut cardboard. It can be seen that there are no limits forced upon the artist.

The inking of the plate is similar to inking in the etching process, but there are a few differences. Since the plate surface tends to be higher in relief, or of deeper intaglio, than usual, the ink should flow well to cover and penetrate these surfaces. Heat cannot be applied to a cardboard plate as in traditional printing to make the ink flow better, and only limited heating can be used under hardboards. Therefore the consistency (viscosity) of the ink is important to achieve a good print. Normal oil-base printing inks can be used if slightly thinned with turpentine or mineral spirits. However, there are collagraph inks produced today that work much better, such as those made by the Leber Ink Company, Seattle. With the help of scrub brushes and cloths, the inks are vigorously rubbed into the plate surface from every direction. Then the ink is wiped off with clean rugs, pelon, toile, etc.

Almost any papers may be used to accept the print image, but they should be somewhat heavier than the thin rice papers sometimes employed with etching. The paper is thoroughly dampened, blotted to remove excess water, placed on the plate, and then run through a press. Almost any type of press can be used, but the collagraph requires considerable pressure and the better the press the more professional the print. I have seen everything used from old washing machine ringers and block-print hand presses to small 3-M presses and professional models. Glen Alps has one of his own design, which is probably the best I have seen for collagraphic purposes. It incorporates many safety features, comes in hand-operated or power-driven models, has a bed of 3 feet, four inches by 5 feet, 6 inches and is used in many private and university studios. (For further information contact Glen Alps Press, 6523 40th Ave. N.E., Seattle, Washington, 98115.)

Alps' direct approach to the plate can be seen in THE OPTICAL SQUARE, Collagraph Plate, Figure 66. The base for the work was Upsom board. The back and edges are covered with polymer medium or shellac so they can easily be wiped clean of ink. The working surface was evenly coated with polymer emulsion in two applications, the second application being brushed on in a contra direction to the first. While the polymer was still wet, ground walnut shells were spread over the entire surface and pressed into the damp polymer with a flat piece of heavy cardboard. When dry, the excess was dusted off. For a more uniform surface Alps sometimes sands the imbedded shell particles with a belt sander.

The circular forms and lines that appear white on the plate were painted over the textured surface with white lacquer. The lacquer is a harder polymer in solution form and the result is an impervious surface that can be wiped clean of ink to produce clean white forms in the print. (Four or five coats of polymer emulsion would accomplish a similar result, but is more time consuming than one coat of lacquer.) A few lines were then cut into the lacquer. This can be done with anything from a matte knife to linoleum tools or a pocket knife.

Figure 67 shows the end result. The blacks are quite intense due to the fact that the fine walnut shell particles hold a great quantity of ink and also because the ink was rubbed into the plate with a four-inch scrub brush. The ink used was *Collagraph Master Black P.M.S.* by Leber Co., Inc. After the damp paper received the print it was stretched by paper-taping to a flat board and allowed to dry.

THE WHITE SQUARE, Figures 68 through 73, is a four-color work by Alps. The original plate for the dark color was developed in much the same manner as for THE OPTICAL SQUARE described above. Flat dark areas are ground walnut shells pressed into wet polymer medium. The flat, light area is the board, covered with medium and otherwise unadorned except for a few lacquer brush strokes. The board prints with a light texture when treated this way. The linear design was achieved by cutting strips of cardboard and attach-

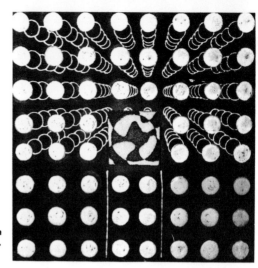

Figure 66. THE OPTICAL SQUARE. Collagraph plate, approximately 24 x 24 inches, by Glen Alps. (Courtesy: the artist.)

ing them with medium. The white cardboard line is lacquer covered, the black is covered with shell particles. The white square is, again, cut cardboard covered with white lacquer. The small shapes are also cardboard cut to match the preliminary design sketch, adhered with polymer emulsion and then covered partially with medium, lacquer, and ground shells. (See overleaf.)

Figure 68 shows the first proof from the original dark plate. As can be seen by comparing this proof with the corrected plate (Figure 69), a painterly, textural area was added to the "Y" shape in the plate after the proof was pulled. This was done by painting on medium with a soft brush and pressing shell particles into the wet medium. This is one of the advantages of collagraphic processes: additions and changes can be directly, almost immediately accomplished.

The red, yellow, and blue of the print is carried on one plate. As can be seen from Figure 70, this is a relief plate as opposed to the dark intaglio plate. Therefore the three colors are printed with one press operation. Cardboard is cut to the color shape and adhered to the base cardboard with

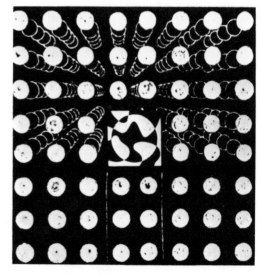

Figure 67. THE OPTICAL SQUARE. Collagraph print.

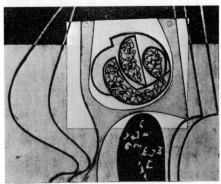

Figure 68. Step 1. Dark print. This is the first proof from the original dark plate, before corrections. Compare with Figure 69.

Figure 69. Step 2. Dark plate, corrected. Note the textural area added to the "Y" shape.

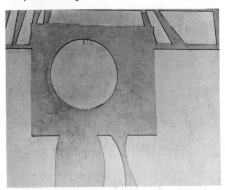

Figure 70. Step 3. Three-color plate.

Figure 71. Step 4. Color stencil.

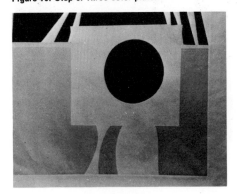

Figure 72. Step 5. Three-color print.

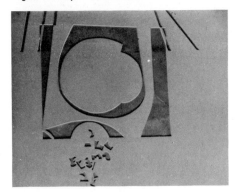

Figure 73. Step 6. Emboss plate.

The finished result of the above technique is reproduced on Color Page 99.

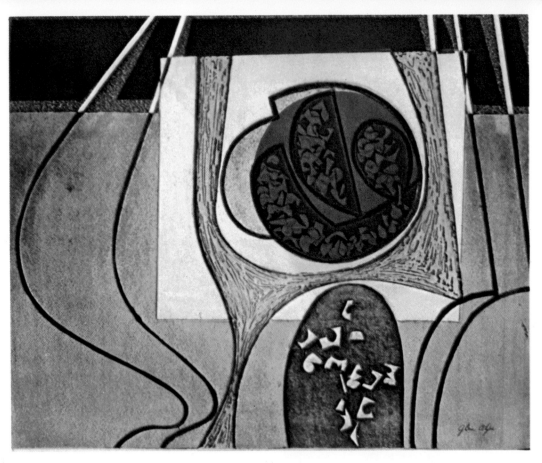

THE WHITE SQUARE, Collagraphy print by Glen Alps. (Courtesy: the artist.) The technique is described and illustrated on pages 96-101.

medium. To prevent the color inks from being wiped onto areas where only the dark color was wanted, a stencil was cut to fit into these "negative" areas. (See Figure 71.) Then three colors were wiped onto the plate and printed as seen in Figure 72. After the colors were dry the print was dampened and the dark color, intaglio plate was overprinted. The print was stretched and allowed to dry

The last step was to emboss the print for a more sensitive and tactile quality. Therefore an embossing plate was prepared by rubbing the original graphic sketch on cardboard to transfer the design and then cutting the desired emboss as seen in Figure 73. The embossing operation, accomplished when the print was dry, was done by pressing the paper into the embossing plate with the fingers, thumb, and palm of the hand. Alps prefers the hand emboss to one achieved by the press because, as he says, "it gives greater sensitivity and variation of depth and sharpness of emboss." The final finished print of THE WHITE SQUARE is reproduced on Color Page 99.

Alps states that any ink, paper, plate material, or binder can be tried and experimented with by anyone who knows the general idea of the procedure involved in the collagraph. He covers a variety of approaches, but in the area of polymers suggests: *polymer gel medium* for gluing on materials, for building-up surfaces and textures of various kinds; *polymer gloss medium* for coating, for gluing, and for build-up by mixing with materials; *polymer modeling paste* for direct build-up of textures, building up various grounds on the plate before any other work begins.

There are some precautions to observe in the above techniques, or, for that matter, in all collagraph build up. First, the artist should keep the plate surfaces low in relief or a problem can develop with torn paper or two areas of greatly contrasting relief not printing correctly. However, if a good press and paper are used this is minimized. The artist should keep in mind that if a piece of tissue paper is adhered to the plate with medium, the outline, as well as the wrinkles of the tissue, will print.

If cut cardboard is used for large, small, or linear shapes the cardboard should be cut at an angle sloping *away from* the top edge of the cut. This type of cut can be seen in the emboss plate, Figure 73. Although not as easily observed in the other plates illustrated, this type of cut is always

Figure 74. UNTITLED COLLAGRAPHY PRINT by George Chavatel. Medium: LIQUITEX with textural additives. (Courtesy: the artist.)

Figure 75. Detail of UNTITLED COLLAGRAPHY PRINT.

used by Alps. If not, the inks will get under the cut forms and deposit too much ink on the print (or even squish out, making a mess) when heavy pressure is applied. Other than this, the artist is quite free as to the technical approach. However, neatness is an advantage, and is almost second nature to the professional printmaker.

Glen Alps' work has been exhibited in all the major museums in the United States and abroad. His work is in many private and public collections and he has received two Ford Foundation Grants. As a teacher, Alps, together with other outstanding artist-teachers, freely shares his technical procedures and achievements. He does not make technique a fetish, nor does he protect his "secrets" as do many who make technique an end in itself. He has produced an excellent color film on the collagraph, which describes the procedure beautifully and is available on a rental or purchase basis from the Glen Alps Press. (See page 96.)

George Chavatel, artist and professor, has also done considerable experimenting with collagraphy. Chavatel uses two different techniques in collag-

raphy. In the first process, he applies a coating of polymer medium to Masonite and, while it is wet, he adds textural materials such as paper towels, gauze, and granular materials in the nature of sand and carbide abrasive powders. Two final coatings of polymer medium insure adhesion.

Chavatel's second collagraphy technique, which uses polymer gesso as a glue and a textural surface, can be seen in Figures 74 and 75, UNTITLED COLLAGRAPHY PRINT.

A "drypoint" effect can be achieved by scratching into a gesso- or modeling-paste-covered plate. Modeling paste can be used to effect a whole plate without added embellishment. If mixed with gel medium (50% gel, 50% modeling paste by volume) the paste will not crack and can be brushed on in a painting technique; without gel, it will crack readily. The brush marks will print when inked and wiped. To vary contrast and decrease absorption of the ink by the paste, polymer gloss medium can be applied in various areas and thicknesses. Of course the paste can be carved or tooled in any manner.

Silk Screen Blockout and Printing

The polymer emulsion mediums may be used as an excellent silk screen blockout liquid. Either the clear or tinted (for clarity) mediums (matte or gloss) may be painted on silk and allowed to dry (within 30 minutes). This, of course, will block out inks in these areas. The design may be drawn directly onto the silk with a relatively hard lead pencil. To remove the blockout use the polymer remover for the particular brand of medium employed.

The printing ink for this type of blockout is polymer jar colors or any water-based ink. Oil- or solvent-based inks cannot be used because they will make the polymer blockout gummy. To every two ounces of paint used add two tablespoons of gloss medium. (See Figure 76, A, B, C, D.) This gives flow to the paint, keeps it from drying too fast, and insures permanency, especially if screening is done on cloth. If the artist finds that the paints dry too fast, a small quantity of Propylene Glycol can be added as a retarder (see page 23).

I do not suggest that polymer emulsions be used as a printing ink for collagraphs, because they dry very quickly and very permanently. Also, they should never be used in block printing by those not initiated in good printing procedures. What usually happens is that the amateur will very quickly and very permanently adhere his paper to the block.

But polymer colors used as ink do give some inherent advantages. The first is the intense and permanent colors that are produced with the paints. Second, the more medium added, the more transparent the colors become. This gives a clarity in overprinting colors and designs impossible with oil-based inks, due to the yellowing nature of the oils or gel additives. With polymer colors multiple transparent-translucent overprints can be made, giving unusual depth of color as well as design and color mutations hard to achieve in any other media. Polymer colors are especially geared to the serigraphy process.

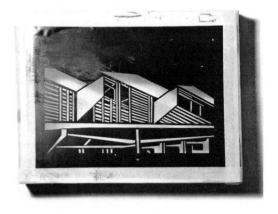

Figure 76A. Step 1.

102

SILK-SCREEN PRINTING
WITH POLYMER EMULSIONS.

Figures 76, A, B, C, D. This series of illustrations shows polymer emulsion color in use as a silk-screen ink. Figure A is the blockout of the screen using cut "contact paper" as the blockout film. This can be employed for a limited run, but pro film is much better and will not release as easily in cleaning procedures. Figure B shows the application of polymer paint to the screen. The paint was thinned with water and a retarder was added. In Figure C the polymer is pulled across the screen with a squeegee. The final, permanent result is seen in Figure D. (Courtesy: Binney and Smith, Inc., Studio.)

Figure 76C. Step 3.

Figure 76B. Step 2.

Figure 76D. The final result.

acetone—a strong and highly volatile solvent. *See* volatile thinners and solvents. Available from chemical suppliers and large drug houses.

acrylic—type of synthetic resin used in making the synthetic paints. Acrylate and methacrylate resins are made by polymerizing esters of acrylic and methacrylic acid.

aggregates—inert materials such as sand, pebbles, Celite, etc., mixed with paints to obtain textures, greater viscosity, or better bonds.

alkyd resins—synthetic resins used especially as surface coatings and with lacquer paints to give characteristics such as durability, non-yellowing, and flexibility.

alla prima—in painting, completion of a work in one sitting.

Aqua-Tec—acrylic emulsion paint line produced in jars and tubes by Bocour Artists Colors, Inc., 552 West 52nd St., New York, N.Y. 10019. Available at art supply stores.

aquatint—a printing technique in which powdered rosin is applied to a metal plate, the plate is heated, and the uncovered part of the metal is etched with acid to produce grainy light and dark masses of various gradations. The parts covered by the rosin remain white when the plate is printed. The plate is cleaned, warmed, inked, wiped, and printed onto paper with a special roller press to produce the aquatint.

aqueous media—any painting media with a water base.

aqueous synthetic media—water-base synthetic media that dry through the evaporation of water and then become impervious to water. *See* polymer emulsion.

asbestine—a type of talc (hydrated magnesium silicate) used to give body to synthetics. It is an inert, fibrous pigment and will give a matte quality to gloss paints as well as slightly tint them.

bas relief—low raised sculpture relief.

binder—the material used to bind together pigment particles in a paint film. *See* medium.

calcium carbonate (known as "whiting") —an inert pigment used to give body and viscosity to synthetic paints as well as oil paints. Paris White is the best grade. It tints the colors and should be used by the artist only, not by manufacturers of synthetic paints. Source: pigment suppliers such as Fezandi and Sperrle, Inc., 103 Lafayette Street, New York, New York.

carborundum—a hard abrasive, usually black in color, and useful in its powdered or granular state as a textural additive to the synthetic paints and as a surface material for producing gray masses in collagraphy prints. Available from large building supply stores, industrial suppliers and, in some cases, from pigment suppliers.

casein—refined curd of milk, which is a strong adhesive. In casein tube colors, a solution of casein in water is emulsified with various gums or oils, different with each manufacturer. Casein is too brittle to use alone as a paint binder.

Celite—a type of diatomaceous earth produced by Johns Manville, Inc. (Sales Corp.: 270 Madison Avenue., New York, New York) and available through large paint stores or building suppliers.

collage—a composition pasted together of materials such as paper, cloth, wood, found materials, etc., usually of contrasting texture and pattern.

collagraph—a print produced from a plate made by collage methods.

copolymer—a polymer made by chemically combining different classes of monomers. For use in an artist's paint this should be a chemical combination of acrylic and vinyl monomers, and the term "copolymer" has that meaning in this book. Just mixing acrylic and polyvinyl polymers together does not produce a copolymer, only a mixture.

The use of "copolymer," as applied by some to the polymer made from various acrylic monomers, is not the accepted meaning in the trade. The word "copolymer" has no virtue whatever in itself, can mean any combination of any kind of monomers having no relation to suitability for use in artist's paints.

damar—a natural gum from a tree grown in the Malay States, bought in crystals and dissolved in turpentine (or purchased already dissolved) to make a picture varnish for oil paintings. It is a soft resin, as opposed to copal, a hard resin. Source: art supply stores.

diatomaceous earth—an inert clay of light, fluffy, absorbent nature used to give body and decrease gloss in synthetic emulsions and solutions. One of the best inert fillers for this purpose. Source: pigment suppliers.

emulsion—the suspension of very small drops of a liquid in another liquid or, in the case of synthetic emulsions, the suspension of minute particles of plastic resin in water. See polymer emulsion.

encaustic—pigments mixed with heated, flowing wax as a medium, painted onto a support and, when dry, fused with a hot "iron."

etching—a printing process in which a metal plate is coated with a wax or varnish ground, lines are scratched into the ground and the plate is immersed in an acid bath which bites or "etches" the exposed lines. The plate is then cleaned, inked, wiped, and printed onto paper with a special roller press to produce the etching.

Eterna—a synthetic emulsion paint line produced by *Casa del Arte, Independencia*, 101-C, Mexico City. It is not available in the United States.

filler—see inert pigment, clays.

fresco—true fresco or *buon fresco* consists of painting into a surface of freshly-spread wet plaster with water-mixed pigments. *Fresco secco* is painting onto a dry plaster wall, which has been wet with lime water, using pigments ground into an aqueous medium such as casein or the polymer emulsions. The term *fresco secco* may also be applied to any painting done on a dry plaster area.

gel medium—a thick, viscous polymer emulsion medium that dries clear. This term has also been applied to a complete variety of gelled mediums for oil painting, completely unsuitable for use with synthetic emulsions. Be sure that the medium discussed is designated for oil or water media to avoid confusion and painting problems.

gesso—traditionally, chalk or some other inert white material bound with glue to use as a white ground on rigid supports; it is not flexible. Synthetic gessos are ready-to-use liquid ground paints that have a polymer emulsion binder and can be used on any support, are flexible and non-yellowing. Synthetic gessos dry and can be painted over with any medium within 30 minutes.

glaze—transparent film of paint made by mixing a small amount of color with a large quantity of medium.

gloss medium—paint medium that dries to a highly reflective, shiny surface. "Polymer medium" and "gloss medium" are the terms used in the synthetic emulsion lines.

gouache—opaque watercolor. All pigments are used in an opaque manner as opposed to traditional transparent watercolor (aquarelle).

ground—the prepared surface upon which a painting is executed; including a "size" (to seal the surface if necessary) and "priming," which are applied to the support to give a tighter surface, a "tooth," to decrease absorbency or to increase luminosity. Grounds are not usually necessary for synthetic media unless special qualities are desired.

Hyplar—a copolymer emulsion paint line produced in jars and tubes by M. Grumbacher, Inc., 460 West 34 St., New York, New York, and available at art supply stores.

impasto—heavy build-ups of thick paint to three-dimensional masses.

industrial polymer emulsions—as referred to in this book: polymer emulsion produced for the industrial trade as basic mediums for house paints, industrial coatings, glues, and fine arts paints. They are unpigmented and at times require many additives to form a paint. Included are acrylics, polyvinyl acetates, and copolymers.

inert pigments (clays)—fine, powdery substances that do not appreciably tint or change the color of a paint when mixed with the paint for purposes of thickening or matting. Among the useful inerts are: asbestine, calcium carbonate, diatomaceous earth, Celite, marble dust, pumice, silica, talc. They can usually be obtained from industrial pigment sources (such as Fezandi and Sperrle Inc., 103 Lafayette Street, New York, New York) and some through drug and building suppliers. If used to excess by paint manufacturers they can become cheapeners or adulterants, but they also impart desirable qualities in specific cases.

lacquer—*traditional:* a painting medium derived from the sap of the sumac tree found in Japan, China, and the Himalayas. It dries to a hard gloss finish. Also a shellac solution made from the resinous substance secreted by a scale insect native to India. *Synthetic:* very quick drying mediums and paints produced chemically for industrial coatings and automobile finishes, which have the same hard gloss finish of traditional lacquers. Their various ingredients of cellulose compounds, synthetic resins, plasticizers, etc., are dissolved in volatile thinners and solvents. Source: paint stores and industrial paint houses.

lacquer thinner—a volatile thinner used to thin or dissolve lacquers. Available at most paint stores.

lean to *fat*—a painting term that is applied to oil painting, describing the rule wherein paints with least oil content (lean) should be applied before paints that contain a larger amount of oil (fat). If this rule is not followed in oil painting the paint film will crack.

linseed oil—a highly purified drying oil, pressed from the seed of the flax plant and used as the medium for oil paints. Available at all art supply stores.

Liquitex—an acrylic polymer emulsion paint line produced in jars and in tubes by Permanent Pigments, Inc., 2700 Highland Avenue, Norwood 12, Ohio. Available at art supply stores and through school supply houses.

Lucite—an acrylic resin produced by E. I. Du Pont de Nemours and Co., Wilmington 98, Delaware. The resin can be dissolved in volatile thinners to produce a paint medium. Small quantities are obtained from Du Pont distributors, large paint stores, or from Almac Plastics, Inc., 600 Broadway, New York 12, New York. For technical information write: E. I. Du Pont de Nemours and Co., 350 Fifth Avenue,

New York 1, New York.

Magna—an acrylic polymer resin-solution paint line, pigmented and sold in standard artist tubes by Bocour Artists' Colors, 552 West 52nd Street, New York 19, New York and available at art supply stores.

Masonite—a commercial, pressed fiber board available at building suppliers. Tempered Masonite has a hard finish; untempered, a soft finish.

matte medium—a painting medium that dries to a flat, non-glare finish.

matte varnish—a final varnish which will not cloud over dark colors and which dries flat. It may also be used as a medium.

medium—the basic liquid binder into which powdered pigments are ground to make a paint. A vehicle. (Plural: media) Mediums or various media may be used with and added to a paint to modify its properties.

mezzotint—printing technique in which carborundum is rubbed between two copper plates to create a rough grain on the copper. The rough copper is polished (burnished) with a piece of steel to create white areas of the design when the plate is inked, wiped, and printed; rough areas produce soft gradations of black to gray.

migration of plasticizer—some of the synthetics (notably the polyvinyls) require chemicals called plasticizers to make them flexible. Many of these plasticizers are deficient in that they sink into the support upon which the paint is applied, or they evaporate. This process in which the plasticizer leaves the paint film is called migration; the paint is left brittle as a result. The length of time a plasticizer takes to migrate varies.

mineral spirits—a volatile thinner used to thin oils and some of the synthetic resins. It is a rectified petroleum product, varies in quality from brand to brand, and dries somewhat faster than turpentine.

modeling paste—in relation to the polymer emulsions, a product made by adding marble dust and other inert material to the polymer medium, producing a heavy bodied "paste" which can be used for impasto and modeling and sculptural techniques.

monomer—the thin, volatile, relatively simple molecular chemical units that are polymerized into non-volatile, solid, and extremely stable polymers.

monoprint—a print taken from a surface that will produce only one print copy. A water-base paint is usually painted onto a repellent surface (such as glass) and paper is placed over the design to make the print.

Nacional NRSF—a wetting agent that helps the dispersion of pigments in aqueous media. Produced by National Aniline Division of Allied Chemical Corporation, Somerville, Mass., or Al-

lied Chemical Corp., New York, New York.

New Masters—a copolymer emulsion paint line packaged in bottles by Hunt Manufacturing Co., 1405 Locust St., Philadelphia, Pa., and available in art supply stores. They also produce *Vanguard I.*

nitrocellulose—cellulose fiber that has been nitrated by drastic treatment with nitric acid. It is soluble in certain organic solvents, and, with modification with flexibilizing plasticizers and with various resins, it makes the well known nitrocellulose lacquers (known also as pyroxylin lacquers). While nitrocellulose lacquers are tough and relatively durable for moderate periods of time, their nitrated structure will eventually cause film disintegration.

organic solvents—chemical liquids that are compounds of carbon and evaporate. They are solvents for (i.e., they dissolve) resins and nitrocellulose. The term usually applies to the stronger or more active solvents such as acetone, tuluol, xylene, ethyl acetate, butanol, methyl isobutyl ketone, etc., rather than the more common and weaker organic solvents such as turpentine and mineral spirits.

oxidation—a chemical action in which a material combines with oxygen. Oils dry by the process of oxidation; a chemical drying process.

paint—a combination of medium (binder, vehicle) and pigment.

papier-mâché—a construction or material made by mixing a binder with paper pulp or paper cuttings.

Perlite—expanded mica. A very lightweight material that can be used for textural additives in paint. It is obtainable at building suppliers.

pigment—a dry, powder substance that imparts its color to a medium but which is not dissolved in the medium. Pigments may be either derived from natural sources or produced chemically, synthetically. Source: art supply stores and companies, and pigment supply companies.

plasticizers—substances that are added to a medium to maintain necessary flexibility or to correct undesirable brittleness.

Plexiglas—acrylic plastic manufactured by Rohm and Haas, Inc., Philadelphia, Penn.

Politec—an acrylic emulsion paint produced in jars by the Politec Co., Calle Tigre No. 24, Mexico 12, D. F., and distributed in the United States by the Politec Co., 425 14th Street, San Francisco, California.

polymer—a compound formed by chemically uniting of like molecules into larger molecules and thereby changing the physical properties of the basic compounds (monomers) without altering its essential composition. Volatile monomers are polymerized into

105

non-volatile and extremely stable polymers.

polymer cement—a sculptural medium made by mixing polymer emulsion with cement and other additives.

polymer emulsion—a water suspension of a synthetic resin to form a paint medium that can suspend pigments in a liquid state, and, upon drying, keep the pigment dispersed as well as protected. "Synthetic emulsion" and "polymer tempera" are terms used to mean the same thing.

polymerization—the process by which a polymer is made. See polymer.

polymer tempera—see polymer emulsion.

polyvinyl acetate (PVA)—a plastic resin of the vinyl family which requires a plasticizer to make it flexible. Vinyl acetate is polymerized by adding peroxides and heating to yield polyvinyl acetate emulsions.

polyesters—a class of synthetic resins that frequently are cast in situ at normal temperatures, activated by small percentage of catalyst. The catalyst is usually volatile and highly toxic.

priming—a coating of white paint (usually white lead) applied to a sized canvas to provide a base for painting as well as for a reflective surface in oil painting. The priming can also be one of synthetic emulsion gesso. The oil priming should not be painted over for four weeks after its application; the synthetic priming can be painted over with oils as soon as it is dry (about twenty minutes). A size must be used with oil priming. No size is required with synthetic priming.

Propylene Glycol—a retarder for polymer emulsions manufactured by Amend Drug and Chemical Co., Inc., New York, New York. Available at local drug stores or chemical supply houses. Use sparingly.

pumice—powdered, volcanic-type rock used for polishing materials and for textural additives in painting and collagraphy. Available at large building suppliers, some paint and pigment suppliers.

pyroxylin—see nitrocellulose.

resin—an organic substance exuded from plants or trees which can be dissolved in volatile solvents to produce a paint medium or varnish which is transparent and water resistant. Resins may be hard or soft, recent (extracted from living trees) or fossil (those dug from the earth, such as copal). Synthetic resins are substances that have properties similar to those in natural resins, but which are made by chemical processes, such as the plastic resins discussed in this book.

resin solution—a resin dissolved in a volatile thinner or organic solvent. Resin solutions are not compatible with water or aqueous media.

Rhoplex AC 33 and AC 34—types of acrylic emulsions produced by Rohm and Haas Co., Philadelphia, Pa. Small quantities can be obtained through their distributors (such as Masco Chemical Co., 58 John Hay Avenue, Kearny, New Jersey.)

serigraph—a fine art, silk-screen process in which designs are made on silk. Color is scraped over the design with a squeegee so the color will print through areas of the silk that have not been blocked out. The technique is a multicolor, multiscreen process that resembles gouache painting. The effects achieved can be very subtle and varied.

Shiva Acrylic—an acrylic emulsion paint line produced in tubes by Shiva Artists Colors, Shiva-Rhodes Building, 10th and Monroe Streets, Paducah, Kentucky. Available at art supply stores.

silica—white or colorless and extremely hard silicon dioxides and the principal constituent of sand, quartz, etc. Silicates are the crystalline, inert pigments with little or no tinting strength, used to give body or impart tooth to a medium.

silverpoint—a drawing technique in which an instrument with a silver point is used to draw on a coated paper to produce a pale, delicate gray line. The Old Masters used this technique and coated their papers with a thin colored ground of powdered bone, mixed with gum water. Today the coating can be synthetic emulsion gesso.

size—a coating given to raw canvas before the priming. It protects the canvas from the harmful effects of the oil paints and gives the canvas a heavier body. An animal glue (or glue gelatine) is used for this purpose.

Soluvar—a resoluble (removable) polymer varnish produced for polymer as well as oil paintings by Permanent Pigments, Inc. See Liquitex.

spackling compound—a plaster-like compound used to patch cracked masonry, plaster, murals, etc., and which can be used to create impasto surfaces when mixed with the polymer emulsions. Source: paint stores and building suppliers.

stabilizer—a chemical used to keep many of the synthetic emulsions in suspension.

stand oil—a thickened linseed oil made by heating the oil in stainless metal containers at a high temperature in the absence of oxygen. It does not yellow as much as linseed oil. Source: art supply stores.

Styrofoam—a rigid plastic foam produced by the Dow Chemical Co. and available at building suppliers and plastic supply houses.

solution media—a painting media made by dissolving resins in volatile thinners.

support—the surface material upon which paint is applied; the canvas, Masonite, board, or paper to which the size and then priming are applied.

synthetic emulsion—see polymer emulsion.

synthetic paint—a paint based on synthetic resin media; either emulsion or solution types.

tempera—a painting medium using either animal (egg) or vegetable (gums such as gum arabic) glues diluted with water—as an emulsion—into which are mixed powdered pigments to form a paint.

toluene (toluol)—see volatile solvents. Source: large paint stores and chemical suppliers.

tooth—a slight roughness of the surface.

toxic thinners—see volatile thinners.

turpentine—distilled gum of pine trees. See volatile solvents.

underpainting—the basic structure or design of the painting, which may be done broadly or in high detail, in black and white, complementary colors, etc., before the final painting or "finish" takes place.

varnish—a solution or emulsion medium for coating finished paintings so they will withstand dampness, grease, dust, damage. They are available in matte and gloss finishes for all media.

vehicle—the medium (either traditional or synthetic) used to "carry" the pigment and other ingredients to make a paint. See also binder, medium.

Vermiculite—expanded mica. A lightweight additive used for textural painting and for use as an aggregate in sculpture. Available at building suppliers.

vinyl—a type of synthetic resin used to make the synthetic paints. Vinyl is usually brittle in paint formulations and requires plasticizers.

volatile thinners or solvents—liquids that completely evaporate from the paint film and usually have pungent, characteristic odors. They are inflammable and frequently highly toxic to the human body if steadily inhaled in high concentration. Acetone, benzene, toluene, xylene and lacquer thinners are the stronger solvents which should only be used in well ventilated areas. Turpentine and mineral spirits are volatile solvents with which all artists are well acquainted and are low in toxicity. They are all used to dissolve resins to make paint solutions or to thin mediums or paints. Available from art supply stores, paint stores, or chemical suppliers.

watercolor—an aqueous medium of water and gum arabic into which powdered pigments are ground. Sometimes a plasticizer, such as glycerin, is used in the paint.

wetting agent—a chemical used in paints to help pigments become "wet" or easily dispersed and ground into the medium.

xylene—see volatile solvent.

INDEX

wide ptg Knife

Gel med.

Bamboo Pens